THE DOMESTIC BLUNDERS OF WOMEN

THE Domestic Blunders of Women

BY

A MERE MAN

WITH NUMEROUS ILLUSTRATIONS BY "YORICK"

LONDON

C. ARTHUR PEARSON LIMITED

HENRIETTA STREET W.C.

1899

MEMBER OF
INDEPENDENT PUBLISHERS GUILD

75 Dargate Road, Yorkletts,
Whitstable, Kent CT5 3AE.
Tel. & Fax: (0227) 274655

Specialist in Facsimile Reproductions

ISBN 0 946014 36 1

A CIP Record for this book is available from the
British Library

Printed and bound by
Whitstable Litho Printers Ltd., Whitstable.

CONTENTS.

INTRODUCTION.

A MERE MAN'S bold and unsparing attack on woman's stronghold in the home provoked at once, as must have been expected, a general uprising of the sex in strenuous defence of their position and capacities.

Some few ranged themselves as his allies; but the greater number pelted him with arrow-flights of "winged words," not always feathered with discretion, not ever pointed with keen logic, but, beyond question, shot with shrewd purpose and determined aim.

Men also joined in the mêlée, and, no doubt, on both sides some shafts hit their mark. Now that the time has come to take a calm view of this field of onset and resistance, it is but fair, in recounting "A Mere

Man's" sweeping charges, to let those who have assisted or withstood him speak also for themselves, even if they are content to condemn him and his views in the spirit of Lucetta in the *Two Gentlemen of Verona :*

> "I have no other but a woman's reason.
> I think him so because I think him so."

Our readers will therefore find at the end of this book a selection of letters, assenting or protesting, solemn or sarcastic, grave or gay, that admirably illustrate the interest already taken by the public in the alleged "Blunders of Women," as set forth by "A Mere Man."

THE DOMESTIC BLUNDERS OF WOMEN.

CHAPTER I.

THINGS IN GENERAL.

THERE would seem to be only two ways to write of women—either to call them angels, with the poets, or to abuse them as the short-legged race with Schopenhauer, or the "slum woman" and the "cow woman" with Sarah Grand. I have no desire to imitate any of these authorities.

My mission is one of sheer pity. I married

my wife because I loved her. I have worked hard all my life because I loved her, and now I am writing this series of papers because I love my daughters who are growing up. I look back on my many years of hard work, during which I have earned a good income, and I ask myself, as a business man should—what have I got for it? My banking account shows me that, though my income has year by year increased, I have no more worldly riches than when I started. My cheque-book proves I have spent less money on myself than I did as a bachelor.

Again, I ask myself: What has become of it? The answer is very plain. It has not gone in luxuries. Pound by pound, and shilling by shilling, it has been expended on rent, taxes, servants, schooling, and tradesmen's books—with a capital "T" and a capital "B." This is not very satisfactory, but I hope I am too good a business-man not to ask myself: Has it been well invested? If I have, so far, only been sinking money, wha am I going to get out of it? In other words, What are my assets, and what are they worth?

My assets are my wife and my daughters. If I do not put a fictitious value on the good-will of love, I have to admit that my wife is not an improving property—that is to say, she is not likely now to become more valu-

able to me than she has been in my home life. My daughters I must set down as a mere speculation. They may or may not turn out well.

Every man has two branches of business. His profession or employment—commonly called his "office"—and his "house." My "office," as I have said, has improved. I am forced to admit my "house has not. *I* manage my "office." My partner manages my "house." In every young business there are bound to be extravagances. But greater perfection in the quality of goods and economy should come with experience in management, and in time the "house" should at least show a profit on paper. When I ask myself, in my hard, business-man way: "Is the 'house' branch of my business better managed?" I am bound to admit, in spite of all the affection I have for my partner, that it is not. Not only is there no more saving, but there is no more comfort; indeed, there is less saving, and less comfort.

The next thing to consider is: Am I any worse off than other business men? In fairness to my partner, I am bound to admit that I am not. My friends all admit that whereas their "offices" bring in more money every year, their "houses" become every year a greater drain, and that they seem to get less and less comfort out of them, despite the fact that their partners have now got several assistants in the shape of growing-up daughters.

A character in "Adam Bede," if I remember right, tells that incomparable housekeeper, Mrs. Poyser, that he believes most functions of life could be much better managed by men than women. I must say, when I come to sit down and think about it, the conviction is forced upon me that he was right. I do not know any detail of domestic life that I, or any man of my acquaintance, could not manage better than women do, but I am open to conviction of the contrary, if any woman is brave enough to come forward and refute me with proof. I do not expect or desire that women should compete with men in the business and work of the world; at the same time, I would not attempt to deny them the right, so long as they can prove their capacity. This is the very thing they are not able to do. There should be nothing simpler in the world than to manage a house, a few servants, and a few children on a regular income. As regards the cooking and servants, men manage restaurants and clubs; as regards children, men manage schools. Yet, where is the house, governed by a woman with nothing else in the wide world to do, which is as comfortably and as profitably managed as these institutions are?

The reasons for all this I have been to some trouble to discover, and, with your permission, I propose to take each knotty point separately, and not only show why women fail in the simplest details of administration, but to prove that any man who could give his time to the subject would manage a house, a few servants, and a few children to much greater advantage than any woman.

It would scarcely be worth while doing this, but for the fact that women may benefit materially by my instruction. I confess I am thinking more of my own wife and daughters than of any benevolent intentions of improving women in general. It may be said that this might, with advantage, be done in the privacy of my own home. A moment's thought will prove the impossibility of any such method. A woman always regards her management of a house as perfect. At any rate, she never permits any father, husband, brother, or son to interfere. Even to offer any advice is always to be met with the stereotyped answer:

"Oh! you men, you think you can manage anything, simply because you can find fault with matters of the difficulties of which you have not the remotest idea. The house is woman's vocation, though we know that old maid's children and bachelor's wives are perfect; and if you were to interfere, I should have all the servants leaving."

This, and much more equally profitless and impractical assertion, every man has heard many and many a time. No! women will not *listen* to reason or brook interference. By carefully watching their habits, however, I have noticed that they will read and believe anything that appears in print.

I have surreptitiously studied the papers which they read for "Advice to Housekeepers." I can easily understand, after reading them, why women fail absolutely in their duties. It is a case of the blind leading the

blind. The papers I refer to are entirely written by women, and women who obviously have no houses or husbands or families to look after, or they would not be writing newspaper articles. The writers of this "advice," which is so carefully perused, seem to regard the duties of women from no more serious point of view than how to make soup out of potato skins and a chop bone; how to trim a hat; how to mend gloves, and how to furnish a house out of old orange or cigar boxes, a few yards of cheap yellow gauze, and a bunch of dyed pampas grass—all of which is mess.

It strikes me that the really serious criticism and counsel which I am prepared to give to women generally, and to my own family in particular, would have a good chance of being brought into the family circle by men in my own state, and of being read and taken to heart by wives and daughters as sadly in need of advice as mine are. Hence this book.

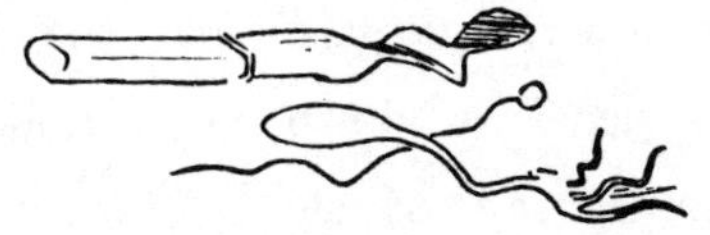

CHAPTER II.

PURCHASING HOUSEHOLD REQUISITES.

MY contention is, that any man could manage his house better than his wife, his mother, his sister or his daughters, or a combination of any of them. Good! Now to the proof.

I want to give women every chance, so I will take their own standard of men. Every woman, at some time or other, has said that the way to a man's heart is down his throat. This is a polite way of saying that men are *gourmets*, if not *gourmands*. I don't believe it, but there may be something in it. Anyway, I accept it for the moment, and it stands to reason that as most men work all their days from the time they are boys till they are old men, and seldom get any more out of it than a cart-horse, merely harness, food, and a bed at night, they have a right to expect that their stable should be comfortable, their bran-mash fit to eat, and their rest undisturbed. It must be accepted that nearly all we earn is spent on our homes and the luxury of our women-folk. What do we get out of it?

All that we ask are comfort and clothes and food. Not a very exacting ambition, surely. The question is, do we get it? Let us see.

The proudest boast of a mother is that her daughter is a thoroughly well-brought-up girl. This may mean she is able to cut out her own clothes, trim her own hats, order a pound of candles, pay her bills with her parent's money, speak French indifferently, and if put to it, cook a chop or boil a potato. To cook a chop well is not very easy—to women—but let us suppose that a woman can cook a chop really well. That is, from the woman's point of view, the very highest point of perfection she can reach, and having cooked a chop well, she is supposed to be absolutely proficient in all branches of her business.

This chop is, like the rib from which she sprang, the root of all evil. A woman always begins a thing from the wrong end. The chop is typical. A woman never thinks that the cooking is absolutely the last stage of the chop, and that she has not the most elementary knowledge of any other stage. A woman to whom this remark was made would say that she knows how to buy the chop. That is precisely what I want to get at. Does any woman know how to buy a chop ?—that is to say, has she the very remotest idea how to buy the best chop for the least amount of money ? What is the procedure ? A woman wants a chop, because a chop is the first thing she thinks of. She goes round to the butcher, and in nine cases out of ten tells him to send her round some nice chops. Just imagine even a woman buying a hat on such a principle!

In the tenth case, the exceptional woman asks the butcher if he has any nice chops. He says "yes," of course. She asks to see them, and possibly says they look too thin, or too fat. In such cases, the butcher says they won't look too thin or too fat when they are cooked, and with this assurance they are ordered. If the husband finds fault with the chops being all fat or all bone, she says they were the best chops the butcher had—as though that was any reason for buying them—and shelters herself further by saying the servant must have spoilt them in the cooking.

An inexperienced husband who asked how much he had to pay for the advantage of eating fat or looking at bone would, in nine cases out of ten, be told that the "book" had not come in yet. In the tenth case, he would be told that Silversides, the butcher, always charged fourteen pence per pound for chops, and further cross-examining would elicit the fact that no allowance was made for bone or

They have only women to deal with.

fat. No wonder that butchers make fortunes. They have only women to deal with, and there isn't a woman living who knows what beef or mutton costs per pound on the field, and what is a fair middleman's or a butcher's profit. It is just the same with fish, poultry, vegetables, groceries, bread, or any of the other requisites of household food. The shop-keeper makes any price he likes, and no woman ever knows what she ought to pay, or thinks of acquiring knowledge to enable her to make a bargain.

And here comes in one of the most extraordinary features of the so-called economical woman. She will willingly pay the butcher for tons of bone and fat in the year, but if you ask why you can't have a cauliflower to make two shillings' worth of tough beef palatable, you will be told cauliflowers are far too dear. Imagining they are at least a guinea a piece, you ask how much they are charging for cauliflowers? You are told fourpence-farthing, or fourpence-halfpenny. Thunderstruck, you ask how much they usually cost, and you are told fourpence, and that no woman who respects herself would dream of paying the extra farthing. Just imagine a woman buying a hat, and saying hat-pins to keep it on her head were too dear.

The fact of the matter is, women have not the least idea of the value of anything—least of all, money. In the first years of their married life, or management of a house, they tell you (afterwards) they were robbed. Women's idea of being robbed consists in trades-people not conspiring to look after the interest of people who do not know their business, but are prepared to accept anything, rather than have the trouble of learning and looking after their own business, and getting the best value for the least amount of money.

In the succeeding years they have picked up a superficial knowledge of what they think are the normal prices, and these they stick to with a pertinacity that, while providing you with joints which are far too large, and are half-wasted, denies you a cauliflower or a carrot because they are a farthing too dear. It is the same with fish. A woman will provide you with three times too much mackerel, costing perhaps three shillings, but will deny you a pound of salmon because its price is half-a-crown.

Women, I have said, have no idea of the value of anything—least of all, money. I shall have further occasion to demonstrate this, so I may now say they have no idea of business. Let me show them how men go about the conducting of the other branch of their business, namely, "the office." I have said that when a woman knows how to cook a chop, she considers she is a perfectly qualified partner for a man of business. This is as false a deduction as that a man who can lay a brick is a qualified architect or builder.

Let me take an example. I would take my own business, only that it would be argued that it was exceptional, and that I was a specialist, and taking an unfair advantage. Of course, all properly conducted businesses are the same, so I will take my publisher's business, so that he, who is my partner in this book, can the better judge of the truth of my general statements, though I may err in detail.

You, sir, are a newspaper proprietor and a publisher of books, and I assume that before you undertook to publish this book you made something like the following calculations. You, no doubt, settled that a certain class of paper was necessary to print it on, and having sent for a paper-maker you asked for his lowest estimate for that class of goods, telling him yours would be a large order, and that you would pay on delivery, or in three months, or in some way most convenient to you both. Having got it, I presume you got other estimates, and took the most advantageous. The same method, I have no doubt, you followed with the printers. Having got your papermaker and your printer, no doubt you set down the rent of your office, the salaries of clerks and the amounts you have to pay me, and, to make a long story short, estimated the cost against the possible revenue from sales. If the first few numbers of one of your enterprises did not answer your expectations, I presume you would set about making alterations, cutting down expenses in one direction, and extending them in another, till you began to see a profit on your investment, and possibly established a sinking fund.

There is no use in proving this too far, because it is what every man does, and every man who has the pluck has tried to explain it to his wife, and he can do so again by giving her this book, if she is disposed to learn and apply it to her own case.

Every woman, when she marries, enters upon a new business, which at once produces a regular income of some kind. It is useless to argue that it does not, because, in that case, a woman simply proves her further unbusinesslike ability by embarking from purely sentimental reasons in a wild-cat speculation, no better than gambling on the turf or the Stock Exchange. Now, how has she been prepared for this venture? Has she studied her subjects thoroughly, so as to avoid being what she calls "robbed" by tradesmen, and has she studied how to cater for the public to which she appeals for support, namely, her husband?

Does she go to a butcher, for example, and ask for his estimate, and when she has got it, say:

"I intend to spend so much a week; I intend to deal with you for a year or more if you give satisfaction, and I pay every week. I know that all these things are considerations to you, and that, as a business man, steady custom and ready money are an advantage to you. Under these circumstances, what will you take off your prices, or what discount will you allow me?"

Is there any man living who can tell me such a thing could not be done?

Is there any woman living who can tell me she has done it?

If so, I shall be glad to hear it, and I think most women will be as surprised as I shall be. Every middle-class house in London burns from fifteen to thirty tons of coal a year. Is there any woman with a small cellar, who has written to the secretary of a coal company and offered to send her cheque for twenty tons of coal, provided he will deliver it as required? Independent of strikes, this would save any fairly large house about £5 a year. Women suffer under the delusion that their custom is too small to make any difference to tradesmen, and they hate and fear nothing more than to change their trades-people. To explain the folly of this, I will relate an incident in my own family life.

Some years ago we moved into a picturesque, but not very thriving, suburb. It has always been my custom to have a fresh roll for my breakfast, the rest of the house preferring toast or bread one day old. One was ordered from the best baker in the district. Morning after morning it arrived late, and, on my insisting on it being delivered in time, it was fetched by one of our servants without my knowledge. One day she forgot, and I discovered the foolish method of pandering to the caprices of the baker. I insisted that a letter of complaint should be written, and the account closed. My wife begged. I was firm. She wept and pleaded that the baker was the only one in the district who could make bread fit to eat. I said I didn't care; I would punish him. My family scoffed, said the baker was richer than we were, and cared nothing about our small account. I said we would see. The letter was written. The account closed. That evening the baker's man waylaid me, and begged for my custom, promising punctuality. I stood to my guns. The next morning the baker called personally, and apologised, and said, as a business man, I was right, but he hoped I would give him another trial. I said I would think about it.

His wife interviewed my wife, and his daughter interviewed my daughters. I had taught them all a lesson, and so I consented

I said I would think about it.

to renew my custom in a month. From that day, till we left, the baker's man altered his round, and my penny roll was never late. Our bread book came to about 4s. a week, but the baker was a good business man, and good business men cannot afford, though they may be richer than their customers, to throw away any business bringing in ten guineas a year. If women would only, as a body, learn this elementary lesson in domestic economy, they would very much lighten their lives, and the lives of everyone who is near and dear to them.

CHAPTER III.

WOMEN'S IGNORANCE OF THE VALUE OF MONEY.

I TRUST that some of my readers will send me some account of the heated arguments which have resulted from my words being discussed, for there never was a man yet who has not "had it all out" with his wife hundreds and hundreds of times. Every woman, however, believes that her husband is the only unreasonable person in the world. The only point in my writing and publishing this book is to show that the scandalous mismanagement of women is a general grievance.

In the last chapter I spoke of the absolute incapacity of women to do their marketing on anything like commercial and economical lines. I think I proved conclusively, to the minds of all men at least, that any business run on the same lines as a "home" is conducted, would result not only in bankruptcy, but in the manager being censured by the Official Receiver for hazardous speculation and reckless extravagance.

I intend now to review the financial capabilities of the feminine gender. I have shown that women have no idea how to spend money. I shall now show they have no capabilities for saving money. This is the root of the whole evil, but it has many developments, as I shall show. The woman who asks her husband for "housekeeping money" simply obtains money under false pretences, for there is such a thing as criminal negligence.

Is it in the experience of any man

that, having given £5 to his wife, he has ever seen the value of a hundred shillings for it? In the first place, is it ever possible to get a proper estimate for "the things" which are to be bought? A woman says she wants "*some*" money. You ask her, how much? She says, she can't tell exactly. Supposing you ask her to make out a list, and supposing you get it. Ask her how much it will all cost. She has not the least idea. Ask her how much each item costs. She cannot tell you. Anxious to get to your business, you say, "How much *about* will they be?" She says, "About £4 15s.," and adds, "It may be a little under, and it may be a little over." In despair, you give her £5.

Intent on getting her into business habits, when you return, you ask her for the change, or perhaps you wait till she wants some more money. In the first instance, she says she remembered when she was out that she owed a little bill, and thought she had better pay it, or that the saucepans wanted renewing—oh, those saucepans!—or she saw some very cheap window-blind muslin, or stockings for the children—oh, those children!

But did you ever see those saucepans, or those stockings? I never did.

In the second instance, she says, "the things" came to a little more than she anticipated. If you have kept, or can recall, the list, and try to get the price of each article out of her, she will get as far as accounting for £4 10s. or £4 15s., but farther than that she cannot remember. If you really want to get to the bottom of the whole business, you should say, "You must have lost the change." An accusation of losing money a woman always resents, with "The idea of such a thing!" She next recollects that she bought herself a pair of gloves. If you suggest she bought gloves a week ago, or that she has her dress allowance, she says, "Of course, if you want me to walk about without gloves, you should say so." As your "saying so" would mean a row, you suggest that 5s. could not be better spent than on gloves, and you mark off your 5s., like the iron cable in the Admiralty report, "Eaten by rats."

But supposing your wife asks for £5, and, it not being convenient to give her more than £2 10s., you again ask her for a list of the "things which are required for the house." If you get it, you will find that more than half the items are not pressing, and so you give her £2 10s., and tell her she must make it go as far as she can. The next day she asks you for the other £2 10s. To make a long story short, you will find that she has bought all the "things" which were not pressing, and that she has left unpurchased all the things that were. Among the former are half a dozen boxes of Snowlight soap, and when you emphasise *half a dozen*, she says, "We cannot have the house without a bit of soap." Oh! that Snowlight soap!

They give a coupon with each box, and for sò many coupons they give the children a set of brown-paper toys. I live in a £60 a-year house, and I have bought enough saucepans —what is the attraction about saucepans? —and Snowlight soap to stock Windsor Castle.

I have bought enough Snowlight Soap to stock Windsor Castle.

It might be going a little too far to say women are absolutely dishonest about money; but it is not going a bit too far to say that they have no idea how hard it is to earn, that they have no idea of its value, that they cannot save it, that they have not the remotest notion how to spend it properly, and that, therefore, they should not be entrusted with either its saving or its spending.

The real fact is, girls are not brought up either to have or to do without money. They cannot estimate the value of anything—not even their own clothes. They cannot keep accounts of money, and are really as much afraid of it as they are of a loaded pistol. It seems like a mere paradox to say women are afraid of money, but their acts suggest this, for their natural inclination seems to be to empty their purses, and a women is never so happy as when she is spending money, not necessarily on articles she wants, or even on herself. She will buy anything, lend or give away any sum, as long as she can get rid of money. There are women who would not run into debt for worlds, who would not part with any of their possessions, but who will get anything for themselves, or give anything away to their acquaintances, so long as they can get rid of actual money which they have in their pockets; and nothing is so common as to hear a woman say: "I thought I might as well buy so-and-so, as I had the money in my pocket."

Women are divided into two classes: the woman who never pays for necessaries, and the woman who never buys anything unless she can pay cash. From the financier's point of view, one system is as bad as the other. Women not only dissipate men's money, but they destroy their credit. I am talking, of course, of middle-class women, who marry middle-class men, who earn their living from week to week, month to month, or year to year. Every man of business is a man of credit. Though, perhaps, only having a £100 in his bank, his bills for £1,000, running over three, six, nine, and twelve months, are readily accepted and handed on as cash. In France, this system prevails even in the home. Owing to the fantastic finance of women, no such thing exists here, and the result is, a man has to keep money for "weekly books," which would be much better employed in his business. The result is long credit and ruinous prices with shopkeepers, or a constant drain

of ready money to the detriment of credit. Women will not understand this. I will explain.

When I was a bachelor, I seldom or never paid cash. If I wanted clothes, or even wine or cigars, I sent out and ordered them. When the bill came in, I always paid something "on account." The result was, my credit was excellent; that is to say, my tradesmen always trusted me, and said of me, "He always pays"; and, besides this, I was never without money in my pocket, and if I were a bit short, nobody was frightened. Since then I have married. My wife has always insisted on paying her weekly books regularly on Saturday. She said it was "her way." She considered it disreputable to run bills, and said that if she sent a cheque on account, people would think we could not pay, and would not trust us, and, worse than all, "would talk." So far, it has not mattered. But, supposing I suddenly wanted all the money I could lay hands on for a business speculation. Do you suppose for one moment that my wife's twenty years of paying the "books" weekly would give us a fortnight's credit for a box of matches, or that our tradesmen would accept such a new departure as a small cheque on account? I say emphatically, "No." Having been paid weekly, they would immediately suspect that

I was "broke," and, as sure as my name is what it is, I should receive a dozen or so County Court summonses.

Thanks, therefore, to my wife's system of maintaining our good name, we are not worth three months' credit, and my name might just as well as not have made a weekly appearance in "Stubbs." The result is, that, whereas "my office" has the reputation of being good for hundreds, "my house," which is managed by my partner, is not good for a £10 note. A further result is, that if I did not keep £40 a month out of my business, I might find I could not get a bit to eat, and would be "the talk" of an entire suburb.

It must be clear, therefore, that, since this absurd system of paying "ready money," and getting no discount, pervades the entire ranks of middle-class England, women are not only conniving at the robbery of their husbands, but are ruining their credit. I have already shown that no woman ever gets a discount for ready money. It may be said that they do not know that they could. It would require very little common sense for them to find it out. They must know—they do know!—that their cooks get it on everything that goes into the kitchen, and that their nurses get it for the very milk that goes into their nurseries. If they only looked at their dressmaker's bills, they would see "A discount of 5 per cent. allowed for cash," stated in red letters. Yet it is to people who cannot put two and two together, who cannot keep money, who do not know how to spend money, who keep no record of what they receive, and have no knowledge of what anything should, or has, cost, to whom we entrust the finances of our homes. Are we not bigger fools, and more to blame, than they are?

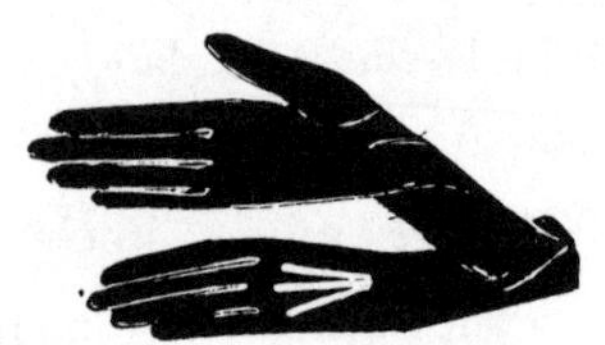

CHAPTER IV.

THE MANAGEMENT OF SERVANTS.

MY one idea in this book is to be strictly fair to women, and not, as so many other writers have done, to attack them unfairly on subjects of vanity, dress, extravagance, or any of the other well-worn topics. To have followed in the lines of my predecessors would, to my mind, have been to prove my own weakness, for we cannot change woman's nature any more than we can man's, and, therefore, to attack women because they are fickle or vain-glorious seems to me as absurd as to attempt to prove that man is not the superior animal because he is, by instinct, fond of cakes and ale. Really, I do not want to attack at all, because it is as natural to me to be fond of women as it is for children to be fond of toys. My real idea is to give women an opportunity for defence, and to prove their strength. It is for this reason that I attack them where they elect to be considered strongest, namely, in their homes. The cry of late years is that women are as good as men, that they have been persecuted and kept under for years, and that, therefore, they should not be expected, in the first years of their emancipation, to be up to competing with men as bread-winners. That is quite reasonable, and, therefore, I do not gird at their mis-management of the political and commercial sides of life.

But the management of the house they have always had, and, as I have said, there they fail hopelessly either to provide comfort, or to spend money in the proper way.

The serpent on the hearth.

I have, so far, shown that the discomforts and extravagances of home are largely due to woman's incapacity to buy in the best markets, and their inability to handle money to the best advantage. I am bound to admit that another great factor in home discomfort is the servants. Nearly all controversies hint at servants being the difficulty, and, needless to say, if I knew my subject at all, I was bound to face the servant question. I will face it, but I fear that, so far from the cause of woman benefiting by the inquiry, I shall hereby prove my allegations against women more conclusively than I have so far done.

Woman's mission is to always put the blame on someone else. Eve began it. She put the blame on the serpent, and her daughters have ever since blamed the serpent on the hearth—the servant. Do not run away with any idea that I am going, for mere love of paradox, to champion servants. A French writer has said, "So many servants, so many spies," and, in my mind, servants are many things worse than spies. But let servants be, as they are, woman's excuse for everything that goes wrong, just as servants put everything on the cat. I accept the gage. For the purposes of argument, we will admit that servants are at the bottom of all the evils of home life. Now let us inquire into that. The first question to ask the woman in

"Who engages the servants?"

the box, who is giving evidence for the defence, is:

"Who engages the servants?"

The answer is "I do." The witness, be it understood, is speaking on behalf of women generally. The next question is:

"Who directs the servants?"

The answer is the same, "I do." Pursuing this line, I ask the mistress:

"From whom do your servants learn their business?"

"From me!"

"And anything they don't know, I may take it, is due to the fact that former mistresses have not taught, or have failed to teach, them?"

"That is so."

"You have heard the expression, 'Like master, like man,' have you not?"

"I have!"

"Have husbands nothing to do with teaching servants their business?"

"Certainly not!"

"What is the proportion of women-servants in a house where two men-servants are kept?"

"Five or six."

"And when the servants are all of one sex, to which sex do they belong?"

"Generally to the female sex."

"Then the proportion of women-servants over men-servants is very large?"

"It is."

"Then, if the entire education, engaging, paying, managing and discharging of servants is carried on by women, and if the proportion of women over men-servants is very large, the entire blame for the unsatisfactory state of the servant question must be due to women?"

The witness does not answer, and, on being pressed, bursts into tears, and finally says:

"It is all the fault of the men!"

I have put this point in the shape of a dialogue, because it is, perhaps, a little shorter and easier to understand. It all amounts to the old saying: "*Qui facit per alium, facit per se!*"

Men, as a rule, have nothing to do with servants, the larger proportion of servants are women, and, therefore, the faults of servants is only another proof that women are incapable of managing another very large section of a necessity which should go to make comfort and economy in the home. But perhaps it is not fair to judge entirely by majorities. Let us look at the exception, which again proves the rule. Bachelors keep their servants, men or women, for years, and, with a few exceptions, always speak of them as treasures. Why is this?

Ask any servant who applies to you for a situation why he or she left his or her last place. The almost invariable answer is: "I could not get on with the mistress." Ask why any gentleman's gentleman, or my lady's maid, left his or her other place, and the answers are always, "The missus, the missus, the missus." As a rule, when a servant gives notice, and is asked by his master why he wishes to leave, the answer is: "I can't satisfy my mistress, sir," or "I can't get on with the cook." Servants very seldom complain that they cannot get on with "the master." It is always "the missus." Again I ask—why is this?

The most unsatisfactory and sulky female servant will always smile and do anything cheerfully for her master, or the young gentlemen of the house, and when she is in one of her tantrums, it is, in nine cases out of

In one of her tantrums.

ten, because she cannot get on with the missus, or the young ladies, or the other female servants—for the complaint of servants is always against what they call "She." "She" is the terror of the servant of either sex, and where there is dissension downstairs, the female servant is always at the bottom of it. Does not all this show that mistresses cannot manage servants, and that female servants cannot manage one another?

The servants of a house cost as much, as a rule, as the rent and taxes, and yet they never give satisfaction, and are never satisfied. Why is this? I could easily find fifty reasons to account for it. The mistress who overworks, the mistress who underworks, the mistress who is unkind, the mistress who is too kind, the mistress who is too strict, the mistress who is not strict enough, the mistress who makes favourites, etc., etc., would all prove fruitful subjects to enlarge upon, were they not too obvious. The remarkable thing about the whole question is, that though money will secure you everything on the earth, no amount of wages will induce servants, as a rule, to stop long in a place. It is a mistake to imagine that servants are independent and love to roam. As a matter of fact, they are terrified to leave, because they never know what character a spiteful mistress may give them, and one bad character means the street. It is the haunting fear of this which makes them, if possible,

The mistress who is overkind.

give notice, before they receive it, for this is their only protection. Is it natural to suppose that any friendless, and homeless, and moneyless creature willingly leaves a good roof, good food, and good wages, to run the chance of meeting a worse mistress? The thing is absurd, for the motto of servants is the not very lofty one of Gervaise:

"To have enough to eat and drink, to work all their lives, to die in their beds, and be buried decently."

When I was a little fellow, I heard a servant say that the fate of a servant was:

"To work while you are young, to beg when you are old, and to go to the devil when you die."

I have never forgotten it.

There is very much to be said on the subject of mistresses and servants—very much more than I have either space or patience for, and there would be very little use in saying it if I had, as it seems all very obvious when you come to think of it, which women apparently never do. But this fact remains. We are as much indebted to servants for the comforts of home life as we are to our wives and daughters. The only difference between the two classes is that some of us are allowed to try and manage our wives and daughters, and some of us succeed, but none of us are ever allowed "to interfere with the servants"; all wives and daughters mismanage them, to our sore discomfort and their own; another thing is that we can get rid of our servants, but not of our wives and daughters, who, I candidly believe, are really the most to blame, though, poor souls, I do believe most of them try.

The fact remains, however, that women arrogate to themselves the management of servants, and prove their incapacity for the task by the deplorable state of the servant market. Men manage shop-girls, waitresses, factory girls, and all sorts of women engaged in their businesses; but men cannot stop at home to manage servants, and if they could, they could not prevent their wives and daughters from interfering. The question is: What is to be done so that we may live in peace when our day's work is done?

It looks like an *impasse*, but it is not. The larger proportion of servants are women, therefore it is women we have to deal with. The real remedy is to promptly sack all your women-servants, and engage men only. Men-servants will cook, make beds, sweep, and wait at table. Why should they not do so for families? They do it in hotels, especially in France, in restaurants, and in the army. Women apparently cannot, or will not, learn, and women appear to be unable to teach them. Men can teach themselves to cook in a very short time, and all the rest is child's play. Yes, the solution of the servant question is to get rid of your women-servants, engage men, and make them entirely answerable to yourselves. Men-servants will cost a little more, but one man can do two women's work. Chinamen make capital servants; so do Hindoos. Why not Englishmen? Ask any Anglo-Indian or his wife what is the one cause of discord in the otherwise happy home, surrounded and served by men, and you will be told that there never was any trouble, except with the *ayah.* If you ask them what is an *ayah,* they will tell you an *ayah* is the one woman-servant in an Indian house, and that she is not an angel.

Why not Englishmen?

CHAPTER V.

THE MISTAKES OF "THE MISSUS."

IT will be in the minds of all my readers that I opened up the question of Servants and Mistresses by showing that, whatever faults servants have, women are responsible for. That, I admit, was an impeachment of "The Missus." I admitted, however, that servants were far from blameless. I shall endeavour to develop this side of the question, and point out some further faults of the servant system, and suggest some remedies.

I showed that servants are what their mistresses make them. Let us see why mistresses make bad servants. To do this, we must get back to the purely business side of life. Here women are again at fault. In every business in the world which is managed by men, and where novices are employed, they are taken as apprentices and are taught their trade. It is owing to the lax way in which women do their work that all servants are more or less amateurs, in the sense that they are incompetent, or, at least, not qualified. I do not suppose that there is a single servant in your employ, fair reader, who could tell you how she acquired the rudiments, to say nothing of the *finesse*, of her trade. If she comes to you as a cook, you will find that, in nine cases out of ten, she commenced as a kitchen-maid, and has only picked up cooking, as Pope says the apothecaries learn medicine, from making up prescriptions, and by experimenting on her unfortunate employers. It is just the same with maids and housemaids and housekeepers and the generality of nurses. Nobody but a woman would set about earning a living in such a way, and nobody but a woman would ever give her a chance. In this, as in most other things, you see the unsuitability of women to manage the little corners of the world which they are pleased to call their "own domain." How is it possible for mistresses who have never learnt to manage a house or to distribute money to the greatest advantage, and servants who have never really learned their duties, to get on together or to cater for the comforts of man?

The result is, almost invariably, the disaster which follows the blind leading, or driving, the blind. It may be said that I am not quite fair in judging mistresses entirely from the standpoint of professional men. Let me, therefore, take another example, which is rather of the accidental order of profession, and has to do with the lighter side of life. Take a man whom fortune, or misfortune, makes a theatrical manager. To be successful he must acquire a knowledge of many things. He has to learn something of literature, something of music, something of painting, something of dresses, something of carpentry, mechanics, finance, acting, and many other things, and not only learn them in a general

The blind leading the blind.

way, but must know exactly how much every little item costs, the price of canvas, nails, wood, glue, needles, silk, printing, etc., etc. That all managers know all these things I am not prepared to admit, but it is quite clear that the man who does not know them invariably fails in the long run, even though he is prepared to employ people who do. I mention this because many women attribute

Why do women fail?

the success of masters, not to their business ability, but to their ability to employ good servants.

This is only an illustration. Let us get back to the subject itself. Why do women fail as employers of labour? First, because they do not know; secondly, because they are too lazy to learn. Women have succeeded, of course, but only where they are thrown on their own resources. As long as men are content to become, so to speak, merely "backers," that is to say, people who provide money to keep up a fad which they call "Home," so long will women let things drift along without taking the trouble to make "Home" a good investment. By this I am forced to explain that I do not mean a good investment from the point of absolutely increasing the revenue, but a good investment from the same point of view that a grouse-moor, or a piece of good fishing, may be a good investment, namely, something that provides a certain amount of pleasure and relaxation. You may pay £100 for a billiard table, and never make anything out of it. But if it is a good billiard table you may get a large amount of amusement out of it, and so regard it as a very good investment.

The absolute chaotic state of the servant

question is due to generations of women who have let things slide. The sooner they return to first principles the better. What are these principles? Go and see how your father, your brother, or your husband manages his business. You will find that it is on precisely the same principles that men have managed their business for generations. Why is domestic service the only profession or trade in the world which is overstocked and detested? Simply because it is the only one over which women preside, and the only one which is villainously mismanaged, to the disadvantage of the mistress and the servant alike. The cause for this is not far to seek. Domestic service is the only labour in the world where the duties and obligations of the employée and employer are not definitely defined. The result is constant friction.

There is but one remedy. There should be the written or printed agreement, which exists in all other paths of business, between the mistress and the servant. I suppose that the first thing I shall be told is that no servant would sign such an agreement. With all respect, I join issue with this statement. If the agreement were not entirely one-sided, every servant in the world would be only too ready to sign it and abide by it. This is proved by the fact that, wherever a union of men or women is formed, the first demand is for definite rules and a definite agreement. An agreement, if properly drawn up, would be for mutual protection. It would shield the servant from being imposed upon, and from being thrown out at the mere whim of a mistress in the tantrums. It would secure for the mistress that the work of her house was properly done, and protection from the neglect and destruction of her property. The present lax system breeds nothing but mistrust rather than confidence. This, as everyone must agree, is the root of dissension. As matters are at present managed, no servant knows exactly what her work is, and she never has any idea that good conduct and faithful service will result in any reward but the kick-out when she is getting to that age when it is not very easy to find a place.

If I were managing a house, and about to engage servants, I would require each person whom I employed to sign an agreement. In this document, of which the servant should have a counterpart, signed by myself, it would be set forth that, in the case of, say, a house-maid, she should properly clean, every day between the hours of so-and-so, certain rooms which would be allotted to her, and for which she would be responsible, and perform such other work as was reasonable and was agreed upon. I should also furnish each servant with an inventory of such property as was in her charge, and when any article was broken or missing I should require her to report the matter at once, and, if the amount of damage was over and above a certain percentage of fair wear and tear, I should possess the right to deduct so much from her wages. On my side, I should pledge myself to employ, and pay her a certain wage for a certain time, the said wage to increase after certain dates if still in my employ. I should further insist on my right to mark her character with such offences as she might be guilty of from time to time, but which should be considered as atoned for

Supposing that your cook got tipsy.

after a certain period of good conduct, and I would pledge myself to substitute for that agreement a character which would correspond with the marking of the agreement at such time as she left my service. For instance, supposing that a cook got tipsy. If she were a good servant, I should be inclined to look over the matter the first time, but I should insist on marking the agreement. This she would naturally agree to, as it would be to her interest to live down her offence by remaining sober for a year, at which time her sin would be considered as purged, and, if she chose to leave then, I should be bound to give her a character saying she had been in my service a year, that she was a good cook, and was clean, economical, honest, and habitually sober.

Besides this, I should take stock every six months. This is usual in all businesses, and it is eminently desirable in the management of a house. Every mistress knows that when anything is missing it is said to have been broken "a long time ago," and, unless some servant has left, it is impossible to discover who was the delinquent, more especially as nobody is responsible. Another thing which is in the experience of all housewives is that there is such a thing as wilful destruction, or what appears to be remarkably like it. The knowledge of this only comes when you engage a new servant. The morning after her arrival she invariably reports, if she is a cook, that "there is nothing in the kitchen,"

There is nothing in the kitchen.

and pots and pans, and everything appertaining to kitchen utensils, have to be replaced. If it is a housemaid, she demonstrates that there are no brushes, that the handle of the dust-pan is broken, that all the blacking is used up, and the dusters are a mass of holes. If it is a parlour-maid, there are no cups, tumblers, or glass-cloths, and she says she finds all the table-cloths and napkins are in a very bad way. Whenever this happens, the mistress always says the last servant "has stolen the things." How true this may be I do not know, but the knowledge comes too late. I have often heard my wife declare that the wilful damage in our house comes to quite £50 a year, and many of her friends aver that this is a very small average.

I do not depart from my original statement that the real fault of all the discomfort and extravagance of "Home" life is due to "the Missus," but I hope I have shown that my eyes are quite open to the servants' share in it. Servants, however, I think, cannot be expected to take much pride where they have no responsibility, and no reward for looking after interests which are not their own. A system which exists in no other branch of life, and which is eminently unsatisfactory where it flourishes, must be in need of some remedy. I make the suggestion modestly, but I am deeply interested in its reception, and I trust mistresses and servants alike will favour me with their opinion as to its utility, and will make suggestions as to further points which might be included in an argument between the parties. That things are in a very bad state nobody can deny. The question is, can we arrive at a solution?

CHAPTER VI.

THE HIGHLY RESPECTABLE PERSON.

WHILE these chapters were appearing in serial form, I received a large number of letters, some of which will be found in this book. Among these is one which I feel I must mention, as it has made me pause and consider carefully whether I should continue this series, or drop the whole subject, and let the world continue in the same haphazard way that women have reduced it to. The letter runs as follows :

"I wish when you wrote that article about

women that you (*sic*), someone, had strangled you; you have made my life a burden to me (through my husband), what with your harness and your bran-mash, etc., and your mutton chops, and so on. There are no words in the English language bad enough that I could throw at you; please close your series at once, as they won't do good at all, and are only making strife in once peaceful homes."

This is signed "An Angry Wife," and I spare my readers the "P.S." It would be easy to sneer at this blotted and illiterate letter; but I am not so hard-hearted as some of my readers may imagine, and I can see that this badly-written letter is stained with tears. There is even a pathos for me in the vulgarity of the postscript, and I am deeply sorry if any words of mine have led some foolish man to apply them too near home for his own and his wife's comfort. My mission is not to make discord, but to preach peace. I want to show women where they fail, so that they may mend their manners, and, if they will only take heed, and their husbands will only be a little patient with them, though there may be little storms, I am sure the sunshine will succeed.

With these few words, and in this hope, I continue, and I take for my subject women's idea of a good servant, or, at least, their idea of a servant they ought to put up with. She is common to all homes, and I am sure all my readers will recognise her under the title of "Such a highly respectable person!"

Was it Sidney Smith—or was it Charles Lamb?—who said there were three sexes—men, women, and parsons? It is I who say that "the highly respectable person" is a distinct breed of biped, which Hobb would have gloried in. She is common to all nations. She is a cross between a chameleon and Proteus. She is sometimes English, sometimes Scotch, and sometimes Irish, but she is not human, for she has no vices, and she apparently was never born, for nobody ever knew "the highly respectable person" when she was young. She came (from where

She will not die.

it would not be polite to say) into the world when she was middle-aged, and, like H. S. Leigh's famous parrot,

> "She'd look beautiful if stuffed,
> And knows it, but she will not die."

As I have said, "the highly respectable person" is possessed of all the virtues. Among these, she is "very willing." If she is employed as nurse, and the cook gets temporarily indisposed, she does not mind going into the kitchen, and doing her best, and you can always rely upon having a dinner served an hour late, which is either half, or three times too much, cooked. She cheerfully washes up such of the dishes and plates as she has not broken, and cleans those knives that scalding water has left handles on. At the end of her week's reign in the lower regions, you discover that the boiler is burned through, and the sink is stopped up. If she comes to you as cook, when you are short-handed, she does not mind doing her best upstairs; she never forgets to mend any china which "comes apart" in her hand, and you can always tell, by the smell and the stains, that she has not forgotten to fill the lamps.

She is a very tidy person. She always carefully puts away anything you want, and you see, by the way your papers are turned over, that your desk has been thoroughly dusted

—round the edges. And she is handy withal. If a chair is broken, you will not find it out at once, as she will make it hold together—till you sit down—by tying it with string, or driving a tenpenny nail through the back, which is "so brittle and old" that it splits. If she has any washing to do, she makes no fuss about it. She waits till you are out, and does it in the bath-room, and when the waste won't act, and the plumber comes and pulls up half the floor, and the force-pipe smothers the ceiling with semi-decayed soap and dirt, you can satisfy yourself that the mischief was as much due to the fluff and hair which *somebody* put in the bath as the fact that "the highly respectable person" forgot that hot water will melt a bar of soap in time if allowed to stand.

But this is only indoors. If a slate is blown off the house, "the highly respectable person" will clamber up through the trap-door, and march about without fear of slipping with her thick boots on the roof, and when she comes down you will know exactly how many slates are broken. If you send her to the butcher's, you may be sure she will pick the meat she thinks is best for you, and if you happen not to like it as much as usual, you will at least know that she did her best in your interests, by finding that she has saved you sixpence. If her mistress wants a certain kind of stuff, and sends her for it, she will never come back empty-handed. If the draper has not the right material or colour, she will bring back the next best thing to it, and if you are so particular as to object to mixing satin and silk, or pink and magenta, why, the shopkeeper will generally allow you to "take it out" in something he has got, and you don't want, say, in six dozen of glass cloths, or something useful, which are sure to come in handy in a year or two.

But what "the highly respectable person" is most careful of, is "Master's things." She always knows where his socks can be bought cheaper than he can buy them for himself, and she has endless suggestions as to what to do with his clothes, or ties and scarfs, which he so foolishly treasures above much newer fashions and colours which can be picked up at sales.

It is needless to say that such a clever, useful person, who is so careful of the interests of her master and mistress, is not adored by the other servants. They, of course, not being "highly respectable persons," have to be carefully watched. Their letters have to be carefully scrutinised, and, if possible, read. Their conversations at the kitchen door with the milkman, or baker, and at the hall door with the postman, are duly noted; their manner of addressing one another, and any words which they may drop have a terrible significance when reported at appropriate moments, and, that they are very foolish persons, is proved by their objecting to be interfered with on every point, and by allowing themselves to be exasperated into telling "the highly respectable person" to mind her own business. That such a state of open revolt should be allowed to continue is, of course, impossible.

At the door with the milkman noted.

Having awakened to the fact that "the highly respectable person" is trusted and honoured in the eyes of her nominal mistress, the rest of the servants, fearing a month's notice and a bad character, take the unfair advantage of protecting themselves, and give warning. It is thus that "the highly respectable person" prevents her master and mistress from being served by bad servants, for everyone must admit that it is much better not to be served at all than by bad servants.

But the greatest of all the qualities of "the highly respectable person" is the fact that she is a dragon of virtue. She has no followers that anybody ever saw or heard of. Nobody calls and asks to see her; she receives no letters that are not in an unmistakable feminine hand; nobody hangs about the gate and whistles, and nobody has ever been seen to raise his hat to her, look after her, or pass her the time of day, in going by. Perhaps, however, an even greater quality is that she wants no Sundays or week-days out, except to go to church, and, although she is strictly religious, she sets her duty above all things, and never demands her right when she thinks it would be in any way inconvenient to her mistress.

Her mission in life is to stick to her

She has to read her mistress's letters.

mistress as long as her mistress will stick to her. To do this thoroughly, she has to read her mistress's letters, and woe betide the mistress who, not being all that she might be, attempts to part with "the highly respectable person," for "the highly respectable person" is as solicitous of the welfare of her mistress as she is of her fellow-servants. To attain this end, she is careful to keep her mistress up to her mark. In the present deplorable state to which generations of women have brought the Servant Market, the mistress is bound, if not to shut her eyes, at any rate, not to look too closely for faults. But this laxity does not suit "the highly respectable person." Her motto is, "Whom the Lord loveth He chasteneth," and "the highly respectable person" has aggregated to herself the *rôle* of social blister. She tells her mistress all she does not wish to know, but, knowing, must notice. She instructs her when the sieves were not scalded, when the pots are not cleaned, when the bread-pan has been allowed to grow over-full, where half a pound of butter has been put away and forgotten, and she leads her round the house to point out where the dusting has been scamped, and turns up the rugs and carpets where yesterday's dust has been hastily hidden. In this way she fans her mistress into perpetual warfare with her servants, and poses, with virtuous pride, as "a highly respectable person" is entitled to pose, as being careful of the welfare and rectitude of her fellow-creatures.

Men, who are unreasonable, and know nothing of what is good for them, as opposed to the luxury of peace and quiet, are no respecters of servants who are "highly respectable," and act as firebrands. They advocate the casting out of the one "highly respectable person," and the keeping of the majority, who are merely human beings, who have "followers," and who want to go out regularly, as they are entitled to do, and they care little how servants behave when they are away from home. These are the lines upon which men conduct their businesses, and this is possibly why their managers, their clerks, and other employés remain for years in their service and work together in harmony. Women are always crying out against their servants. Does any lady or gentleman want a "highly respectable person" with all the above advantages? I know one, at least, whom I shall be only too pleased to recommend to any master or mistress who has not experienced such a luxury, and I promise to ask no questions. If my readers know of any more, I shall be glad if they will write. Don't all speak at once.

Don't all speak at once.

CHAPTER VII.

THE DOMESTIC INFERNO.

AS the nursery upstairs is generally admitted to be the heaven of our homes, so the kitchen ably takes up the position of—the other place. It is there that all the mischief of the house is hatched, and I must say I think the mistress of the house is largely responsible for its sins. On the few occasions when a man visits it (for instance, when he comes back late, and finds the servants have forgotten to lay any bread, or the fire has gone out, and some sticks are wanted), he is, as a rule, absolutely appalled at its dirt and disorder.

It is true that the stove may be bright, and that the dresser may look very clean with its rows of plates, but if he has to look deeper, what a perfect rag-and-bone shop the whole place is! Only let him peep into the cupboards, only let him open the drawer of the kitchen table, or the dresser, and he will be perfectly horrified to find that his wife allows such a mass of heterogeneous matter to be collected. I will spare my readers a picture of it—let them go and see for themselves. There is only one question I should like to have answered, and that is: Why is it that the drawers in a dresser never have any handles? I am not merely trying to provide the followers of Vilon with a efrain for a *ballade.* I ask in the interest of our best knives, our forks, and skewers, that break and twist themselves out of all shape in their efforts to open the drawers of dressers.

I do not think I am overstating it when I say that if wives would only keep handles on the drawers of their dresser, they would save their husbands £20 a year, which, during twenty years of married life, amounts to £400.

This brings me to the appalling misuse which all the articles in the kitchen are put to. Every trade has its list of necessary tools, and everyone knows that there is not a mechanic in the world who requires to be so fully supplied with plant as a cook, and that there is no skilled workman who puts it to such bad use. With a trowel and a mortar-board, a bricklayer will build a house—indeed, several houses; with a few chisels and a hammer, a stonemason will decorate the side of a cathedral, and perhaps the carpenter is the only skilled labourer who requires anything like so much plant as a cook. She is never happy, and always ready with a string of excuses, till she is provided with a whole houseful of things, which she declares are absolutely essential to the cooking of exceedingly plain fare.

She must have rows of saucepans, ranging from the very biggest to the very smallest,

and everything else in proportion, and as soon as she is provided with them, her fancy settles upon particular saucepans and pans, which she keeps in constant use till they are destroyed. Every man knows that five pairs of boots or five suits of clothes will last longer by being worn alternately than by being hacked out separately; but the mistress never insists upon this system being applied to kitchen utensils. No cook will be happy till she is provided with a meat chopper and a meat saw, but when she has got them, sh prefers to use the best carvers. Whoever heard of a carpenter turning screws with his chisel, or using his pincers to drive nails with?

This will probably send my strong-minded readers into hysterics, but can they deny that cooks persistently use one spot in a sieve till they have rubbed a hole in it, and that generally a cook will devote the first thing which comes to her hand to a use for which it was never intended, and that this system leads to great damage? If they do, I should like to ask them to account for the number of knives which are broken, and to ask them if they ever in their lives saw a knife broken by proper use in the dining-room? It stands to reason, first, that I cannot go through the misuses which every article in the kitchen is put to—such should not be necessary, and is certainly impossible in the space which I mean this book to occupy; and secondly, that as "A Mere Man," away all day at my business, I could not possibly be expected to know; but most sensible women must admit, if they think over it carefully, that the annual renewals of a kitchen are out of all proportion.

This being so, how should it be dealt with? Well, most men of business set aside a certain amount of their incomes for what we call, on our balance-sheets, depreciation of plant. I wonder how many women there are who make any such provision in their own particular business, Home? I wonder if there is one single one who is long-headed enough to have ever thought of such a thing, and I wonder how many there are who have ever dreamed of a yearly or half-yearly "stock-taking"?

Do you know, my fair readers, that yours is the only business in the world which is not conducted on these principles, and do you know that yours are the only servants in the world who object to be charged with deficiencies over and above a certain reasonable amount? Do you know that where servants are employed in similar pursuits by men—I refer more particularly now to waiters and barmaids, etc.—that there is such a thing as a breakage fund, to which all subscribe willingly, and that any surplus is devoted to the benefit of all concerned? Now, do you not think it would be well if you established such a system? Do you not think it would make your servants more careful, and you much richer? I am sure you do, and, this being so, I counsel all housekeepers to put it in practice.

But I must get on to even a more important subject of waste than this. There is, perhaps, no more serious expense in a household than coal. It behoves you to be most careful of its consumption. To do you justice, in many ways you are. You will regulate exactly the amount of coal you use upstairs. You put off having fires for your own comfort as long as you can, and you economise by persuading your family to make one fire do for as many as possible. This shows you are not blind to the terrible expense of coal. But I fear me that, while you are sparing at one end, you are spending at the other.

But there are ways to save coal; that is to say, there is a way to prevent it being wasted. In most middle-class houses, the kitchen has to provide breakfast, middle-day dinner or luncheon, a cup of tea at five o'clock, and dinner. To do this, it is necessary, according to the cook, to keep up a roaring furnace, that would roast an ox or melt enough iron to make a good-sized gun, from half-past six in the morning to close on ten o'clock at night—fifteen and a-half hours. There is no good in going into any elaborate explanations as to how to avoid this. Everybody knows as well as I do—but no woman takes the trouble to see that the cook really slacks down her fire. Of course, everybody will jump to the front, and say she and every other mistress does see to the kitchen fire, but equally, of course, they do nothing of the kind. If you don't believe me, take down your own file, and look at your own year's bill for coal. As a matter of fact, your cook

Look at your bill for coal.

ought not to burn more coal in winter than in summer. As a rule, she burns three times as much. Some cooks are clever enough to hide this by making up the surplus from the better coal. Nothing, however, alters the fact that the real practical cooking of a house —in which I do not include making a cup of tea—does not begin till mid-day at earliest, and is over by 9.30 at latest. In other words, a really good fire is required for about four hours, yet the sparks fly upwards for some sixteen hours.

I expect that I shall have plenty of people writing to say they have tried gas, and found it was no saving at all, as they burned just as much coal as ever. With these persons I quite agree. In fact, I will go further; I should not be surprised to find that it proved infinitely more expensive, because, of course, if you still keep a fire burning from 6.30 a.m. to 10 p.m., and gas besides, there is not much chance for economy to come in.

There is much more to be said about women's sins in the direction of the kitchen, but they belong more particularly to the larder, and I will treat of them under that head. There is no good in taking too many things together.

CHAPTER VIII.

THE BOTTOMLESS PIT.

SINCE writing my last chapter, and thinking out my present one, I went up to our Free Library, and got out the Slang Dictionary. I was anxious to find out why the abode of thieves is called a Thieves' *Kitchen*. I could not discover any reference to it, and I have not been able to make out what led to the Infernal regions being placed by popular assent under our feet. The appropriateness of the superstition seems to have been too obvious for anyone to bother inquiring into.

The basement has as many departments as

Dante's Inferno. We have looked into the kitchen and the coal hole, and found them pretty bad. But there is one place where the mistress of a house wastes less time and more money than in either. It is a popular delusion that every woman regularly visits her larder. In a large country-house, where it is roomy and light, she does in the summer, because it is cooler than the kitchen. But a comparatively small number of middle-class women live in large country-houses, and, as a rule, in towns and small houses, the larder is a dark cupboard under the stairs, and a housekeeper generally has to take the cook's word for its contents. But, however all this may be, even all those who visit it regularly, and take a candle with them, do so at entirely the wrong time, as I mean to show later on.

The upstairs meals, as a rule, consist of breakfast, lunch, and dinner, where there is a late dinner. I do not know how many women are aware of the fact, but

I am sure not one man in a thousand knows that his servants have just double that number of meals. The very first thing which every servant in the world does--long before you are called—is to make herself tea. This is followed by the necessary breakfast, and scarcely has the mistress left her kitchen, after giving her orders, than every servant lays aside his or her work, and proceeds to partake of a meal which takes its name from the hour at which it is held. "Elevens," for such it is called, consists of a hurried snack, at which the domestic locusts devour all they can lay hands on. Under ordinary circumstances, it would not be necessary to say that a meal could not take place unless there was something to eat. This, however, does not seem to have struck the women of the last eighteen hundred and ninety-eight years. "Elevens" are not calculated for by mistresses, but they are provided for by the chief brigand—the cook. How is this done so that the mistress will not miss the food?

Simply by abstracting it from the larder before the mistress makes her inspection.

Most of the wasteful over-eating and pilfering of servants is due to giving the cook discretion as to what the domestics shall have for their supper. Everything in the way of food that disappears is accounted for by saying, "The servants had it for their supper," and there is no going behind it. I admit this evil is a very difficult one to cope with, and I will state the other side. Where the rigid law of bread and cheese for the servants' supper exists, great expense and waste ensue. Servants like nothing better than to eat themselves as nearly sick as possible, and the servant who eats a quarter of a pound of cheese, and half a loaf of bread, every night, to say nothing of ends of butter, costs something, I can tell you, more especially as you get no credit for the pieces of steak, odd cutlets, ends of pudding, and scraps generally, which become the cook's perquisites, and when she cannot dispose of them in this way are allowed to go bad, or deliberately thrown upon the kitchen fire and burned. The generally-disorganised state to which the kitchen and larder have been allowed to come is so appalling that one hardly knows what to tackle first.

In a business managed by men, say a shoemaker's, if a servant were caught systematically carrying out ends of leather, wax, hemp, nails, etc., he would be handed over to a policeman, and would get six months' hard labour; but, owing to the absolutely unbusiness-like way in which women manage their servants, the cook claims "perquisites" as her right, and disposes of buckets full of good food for cash, the butler bags the bottles, etc., the housemaid the candle-ends, medicine bottles, soap, etc., and she and the lady's maid, like the butler and footman, divide the clothes. I cannot spare the space to more than hint at the wholesale household robbery which goes on under the very eyes of women who, all the time, are expected, and profess to be, looking after the comfort and economy of men. It is a hard word to use, but most women simply connive at the robbery of servants, and if the real facts ever dawn upon them, they console their consciences by saying, "Oh, well, anything for a quiet life!" Apart from the upstairs peculations, is there a woman living who does not know—for there is no excuse for her not knowing—that "the weekly char" regularly carries off a mysterious bundle which she did not bring in, and that she is simply a go-between for the thieves without and the thieves within?

To dismiss this painful subject, as I have said, the evils arising from "the servants' supper" are very difficult to solve. Of two evils, however, choose the lesser. It is better economy to let the servants steal and eat the good food than that the ends of fish, poultry, and game, should be thrown upon the kitchen fire; but, whatever you do, on no account ever permit the existence of what is called "the pig-tub." Once you allow such an institution, you set up for yourself a yawning abyss, which devours everything which the cook can steal from the servants and yourselves. "The pig-tub" is the direct product of the false economy of daily marketing. If you market daily, the result is odd quantities of everything, all of which go into "the pig-tub," and, as a matter of fact, there is nowhere else to put them, for it seems difficult to persuade English women to persist on the setting up of a stock-pot, which is an institution in every French establishment. There ought not to be a single house, or flat, however humble, where you ought not to be able to get, at five minutes' notice, a fine bowl of soup without expending one sixpence on gravy, beef, or vegetables. Into this should go every scrap of meat, fat, fowl, and all your spare gravy, your odd carrots, and half onions. Soup in this country is looked upon by women as an expensive luxury, instead of which it should be a staple dish in every humble home of the lower classes. But I have so much to say that I am drifting away again.

It is a popular fallacy amongst women that they must buy their vegetables fresh, and fresh every day, and this is their argument against purchasing large quantities, which would very much save their pockets. As a matter of fact, three-quarters of the vegetables used in a middle-class house are not, and do not, require to be fresh. Take, for example, potatoes, turnips, carrots, onions, beetroots, celery for soup, leeks, cabbages, and cauliflowers, etc., etc. You are not foolish enough, I hope, to suppose that your greengrocer digs, pulls, or cuts these every day for your especial edifications. If you do, think so no longer, and amend your ways. Even the last two, cabbages and cauliflowers keep four or five days, and preserve whatever freshness they require much better in your cool, clean—you see, I am giving you all credit—larder than in a stuffy greengrocer's shop.

CHAPTER IX.

CUPBOARD SKELETONS.

IN my last chapter I was about to condemn the butcher to be, as his trade demands, "hung," drawn, and four-quartered, but I thought it best to start again fresh. The butcher owing to his trade, is looked upon as a sanguinary scoundrel of the worst order. I never knew but one butcher at all intimately, and he was in a big way of business in the wholesale trade, but he told me this was the popular belief. He was very much down on authors who referred disrespectfully to butchers. He took this very much to heart, and went on to demonstrate to me that all the great men of the world had been, or had sprung from, butchers, even Shakespeare, and that he was perhaps the worst. I am sure nothing else would have made him read Shakespeare, which, by the way, he knew very well, as far as the quotations about butchers went, at any rate. But there is an old superstition in favour of a man who breaks his rope being allowed to go free and repent, or hang *himself*, if he is anxious to die suddenly. I have no more space to spend on the butcher, and so to the next man in the tumbril.

This is the gentleman who has long figured in history as "Honest John Grist," the baker. I suppose it is on account of his white cap and apron, and the general flouriness of his appearance, that the baker is universally regarded as a bluff, honest fellow. He isn't! He is a thief of the worst order, and he grows fat on his flour-bags, and rich on his rascalities. The baker is the direct product of the lax way in which women manage their business. He not only adulterates his bread with every deleterious matter he can lay his hands upon, but he has established it as a recognised custom of his trade—against which the law has no powers—that he is allowed to receive full money for short weight. The law says you shall have full weight if you demand it, but if you don't specially stipulate that you require your fourpenny loaf or your penny roll to be worth half the money you pay for it, you must not expect it, nor complain.

But how many women, except those of the very poor class, do this? Not one in a thousand. In spite of this already heavy tax on your pockets, there is scarcely any article of household use which is so wasted as bread. I do not deny that bread is a thing for which an absolutely fixed order cannot always be given. When you are "expecting people," you have to provide for them; some days an extra quantity is used in cooking, as, for instance, in crumbs, toast, puddings, etc. But, over and above this, there is far too great a margin which goes to waste. Every bread-pan in the kingdom is half-full of crusts and ends of half and three-quartern loaves, which are allowed to go to waste. They are allowed to get hard, and are thrown, unless given, away. In this matter your most honest servant has no compunction. She, who will not steal a penny or let anyone else do so, will cheerfully give away pounds of meat and bread to every

beggar who comes to the kitchen door, even if there were ten a day. This is not charity, for everyone knows, or ought to know, that beggars do not want bread, and only throw it over the first paling, or into the first garden they come across. If you don't believe me, have them watched, and see for yourself.

I reckon that, as a rule, seven quartern loaves a week ought to provide bread for a household of six. In other words, your baker's bill ought not to be more than three shillings a week. How often is it ever under twice that sum? Of course, there are pastry and cakes. I have nothing to say against this. Then I shall be told there is flour, which is extensively used in cooking. I know there is. But why is there flour on the baker's book? Do you not know, gentle ladies, who will so abuse me for opening your eyes, that there is such a place as a corn chandler's? Perhaps you have never taken the trouble to find this out, or, if you have, perhaps it has never struck you to inquire why there are two tradesmen of different appellations in the same district who sell the same goods. I will tell you. The flour which you buy from the baker costs you twenty-five per cent. more than the same quality at the corn chandler's. Perhaps you don't care to save threepence in the shilling. I think I heard you say, "It is too much trouble." Yes, I thought so. Perhaps some will write and say that no woman in her senses ever thinks of buying flour from the baker. In that case, perhaps somebody will tell me why bakers sell flour, and whether all those small square bags which I see in the window are only, like the big blue and red bottles in the chemist's, for ornament.

It may be agreed that the robberies of the baker cannot be laid at the door of the mistress. There is something in this, but, like most general statements—my own included—it is not quite, that is to say, entirely, true. The mistress is responsible for all that goes wrong, and the baker, as well as the butcher, is an incentive to the nefarious practice of perquisites. Every mistress who keeps her senses on the alert must know that her baker's and her butcher's books contain items which never see the inside of her house, and that the cook calmly passes eight-pound joints to be charged as ten, and neglects to change loaves, so hat she may receive her miserable commission, which is a direct incentive to robbery, for which tradesmen should get long terms of hard labour.

This brings me to an almost more important factor in the pilfering line. I refer to the

Ought to get terms of hard labour.

grocer's book. I must assume that by now the pernicious habit of the grocer's man calling daily for orders has passed away. In the old days this form of swindle was pretty generally adopted. Every day the grocer's man called, and stood at your kitchen door and suggested to the cook a variety of things which she did not want, but in the ordering of which she took a certain pride and profit. Anyway, whatever the reason, she could not find it in her heart to say "No," and saying "Yes" made the grocer's man so much more polite, and the plunder hurt no one but the sworn enemy of all servants—She. With the introduction of the Stores, however, I believe the daily ordering has dwindled. But still the grocer's book is the Maelstrom of Mistresses. Can anybody answer this to her own satisfaction?

In a really well-kept-up house, where money is plentiful, where pence are not of much importance, and where a good deal of general well living and entertaining is kept up, the monthly book at the grocer's amounts to about £2, and this includes numbers of things which are not in daily use, such as angelica, pistachio nuts, flavouring and colouring matter (such as vanilla, cochineal, etc.), truffles, candied fruits, etc. Now, will anyone explain to me why the grocer's book of a much less ambitious establishment, where pence, not pounds, are of importance, and entertaining and good living are not kept up, is seldom lower than ten shillings, and is frequently as high as fourteen shillings, a week? If any of you have such a book, and if you are not afraid to look at it, you will find that there are no truffles, candied fruits, etc., set down there, but only such homely items as wood, raisins, matches, sugar, jam, etc.

I have already inveighed against the weekly book. Such private arguments as I have had have not altered my views, and I will tell you why. Where a weekly book is kept—that is to say, where a weekly order is given—the cook always, designedly or otherwise, forgets something, generally a great many things, and, at the end of the week, you find these "had to be fetched in a hurry," and your book is bigger than you expected. Another reason for extravagance is that, where a weekly order is given, the items in the store cupboard are few, and as a result, the mistress does not keep it locked or give out the things as they are wanted. The result is that the cook makes a point of using up or wasting everything that it contains, and the mistress only thinks, when she sees the empty cupboard, how clever and economical she is not to have ordered too much. Take my advice, and take it quickly. At once institute a monthly order, see that everything is delivered, check it over as it is put in the store, and put the key in your pocket. This will save you a great deal of trouble, and a great deal of money, and you will find your table is better furnished, and that you are living better for very much less money.

You may well ask, how can this be? In the first place, you can buy large quantities cheaper than you can small quantities. Secondly, your order being a larger and more important matter, you will do it more carefully, and will write it down. Thirdly, you may be induced to keep the list for reference, and you will see that what you have ordered is delivered, and that you get the benefit of what is over. You have no idea what a difference it will make till you try it. Your wood, jam, raisins, rice, sugar, etc., may remain much the same after a few months, but you will find you will save on hundreds of boxes of matches—which were thrown on the fire—and that you always have in hand plenty of truffles, dessert, anchovies, sardines, spices, and all the etceteras which cost so much, and disappear so quickly, but which have to be in a house not so much for daily use as when required for an emergency.

I am always coming back, like a maker of *ballades*, to the same *refrain*. In all businesses managed by men, no order is given or accepted without a written check. If you want really to manage your house on anything like business principles, to save money, and have a good time, go round to a small local printer, and get him to make up for you—they will only cost you about ten shillings—ten books, containing one hundred forms each, which you should fill up (as in *italics*) whenever you give an order, something like the following:

…………, 1899.

To ……………

Kindly supply to

148, St. Anne's Road,
Putney, S.W.

……………………………………

……………………………………

……………………………………

……………………………………

NO CHARGE WILL BE RECOGNISED UNLESS A SIGNED ORDER CAN BE PRODUCED.

Nov. 1st, 1899.

To *J. Spriggins.*

Kindly supply to
148, St. Anne's Road,
Putney, S.W.

5 *lbs. Best Candles,*
6 *lbs. Brown Sugar,*
8 *bars Primrose Soap,*
3 *tins Blacking, etc.*

(Signed)

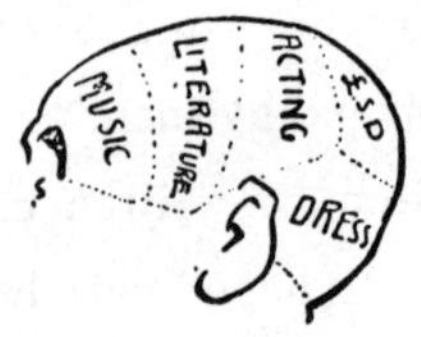

CHAPTER X.

THE MANAGEMENT OF CHILDREN.

I AM now going to offer some criticisms which I know will be resented far more than anything I have so far written, and my only hope is that what I say will do some good.

I have shown that the whole system is wrong, that all the accepted ideas of management are grotesque, and that women have no idea how to save, or to spend, money, and that, therefore, they should not be entrusted with it. Having done this, and it having been admitted I have proved my case, let me hope women will profit by my advice, and mend their ways. But the management of children is a more serious business, and, though I am sorry to say it, I am convinced that women are more ignorant of the management of their nurseries than of any other parts of their houses. Perhaps some statistically-inclined correspondent will kindly give us a statement of the annual mortality of children. Personally, I do not know it, but I believe it to be enormous, so enormous indeed as to be out of all proportion to any other death-rate known. Large as it may be proved to be, it will not surprise me half as much as that it is not twice as large, for I know of no children who do not surprise me when they survive the treatment which they receive from their fond but foolish mothers, and the servants to whose care they are left.

Is there any married woman living who can put her hand upon her heart and truthfully say that, when her first baby was born, she had the very slightest idea as to what ought to be done with it? Women have not the most elementary ideas as to how to take care of themselves. If this were a medical book, I could show that there is hardly a girl living who, between the age of fifteen and her marriage, does not court her own death many times a year. But this is not a medical book and I will content myself by saying that most wives owe any health they may have to the persistent interference of their husbands. I am no advocate of what is wrongly called "rational" costume. This means, generally, giving up skirts, and nonsense of that kind. Neither am I going to run my head against the stone wall of corsets. Personally, I not only like girls to wear stays, but I believe they are a great support to women, but this does not mean that I advocate tight-lacing any more than I do tight boots. But is there any sane person who will argue that half a yard of cambric is a rational costume on a cold winter's day? I do not wish to pursue this subject further than to point out that it is to women, who have such extraordinary ideas of clothing themselves, that the costuming of children is left.

There are three things, I take it, which are material to the health of young children, namely, warmth, air and exercise, and food. I do not think that there is one of them which women understand; but let us take them one at a time. When a baby is born, as everyone knows, it is swathed in flannel, and kept in long clothes. So far, so good. But the first idea of women seems to be to see how soon they can lay aside these sensible garments for a diabolical period, which is called being "short-coated." Short-coating means nothing more nor less than stripping the child stark naked from the waist down, and putting it to crawl about in the place where draughts most do congregate, namely, on the floor. This, too, is the costume in which the child is carried about the house and into the streets. When one comes to write it down, it seems scarcely credible; but such slaves are women to tradition, that hundreds of thousands of children are stripped halt-naked when they are six months old, and remain so, in the case of boys, till they go into knickers, and in the case of girls till they are eight or nine, and even after unless they themselves get sense or husbands.

No wonder, indeed, that infant mortality is so large. I shall never forget being told by my wife, with tears, what a terrible thing it was that her first baby had got cold, and that that meant having a cold all the winter. This had been told to her by the nurse, for the nurse said the same thing when I went upstairs. I found the poor child crawling about the floor in a costume which is best described by saying that it was that of a *première danseuse*, only more scanty. From the waist downwards the child had nothing on but skirts a few inches long, and a pair of short cotton socks. I soon sent out for some yards of flannel, built the fire half-way up the chimney, kept the child in bed on hot drinks, and within a few days—despite what was called "such a terribly weakening treatment"—the child was quite well.

Despite "the marvellous way in which baby shook off the cold"—as the cure was called—the women fought hard to restore the inhuman garments from which I had rescued it. I insisted on the poor little legs being kept swathed in flannel, and although I was told it was most terribly weakening, and was given every other mad reason for sacrificing the child to the convenience of the nurse, "the baby" remained so till he went into knickers and long stockings, and to-day he is pretty sturdy on his pins in a football scrimmage. Now, don't let every woman write and say that children are not kept half-naked from the time they are six months old—for such is not the truth. They are; and that such a practice exists is nothing short of criminal negligence.

I don't mean to say that women mean to be cruel. I don't think they do. They simply don't think what they are doing and allowing to be done. If you suggested taking "the baby" out without its cap, to say nothing of stripping it to the waist, they would think you mad; but it never occurs to them that the exposure of the pit of the stomach to the winds of heaven is five times as dangerous. If these facts are true, and I shall be surprised if they can be combated, how can women contend that they manage children better than men would? How can they contend that they have the very slightest idea of how to manage children at all?

But I do not wish to be too dogmatic. The absurd custom of stripping children half-naked, and being surprised and crying floods of tears when they die, must surely have some champions who can give some reason for what seems to most lay minds sheer cruelty or mere ignorance. If there be such, let them now speak up, to my undoing.

Everything a woman knows, or is supposed to know, she credits the rest of the world with being entirely ignorant of. This is my point. Why should women be the only persons who are believed to be able to take care of children? As a matter of fact, a woman, left to herself, generally nearly kills her child, and then rushes off to fetch the doctor—a man, mind you—to get her out of the awful mess which she has got herself into. I know I shall be attacked for even daring to touch upon the subject of children. The butcher, the baker, and the candlestick maker, perhaps —but children! What can a man know of children? I can imagine every second woman in the land saying this. But the point we have to consider is—What do women know of children?

Now, it must be admitted that women have the entire management of children. What is the result? The plague of London hardly equalled the present infant mortality of London alone. Why is this? Why do more children die every year than calves or lambs, or kittens, or puppies, or anything else? I don't say there is no reason. I want you to tell me, and to prove to me if you can, that it is for any other reason in the world except because they are managed by women. That's what I want to believe if I can, but frankly, I don't believe it. I don't believe women have the very slightest idea how children should be taken care of. As I have said, all they want is proper food, reasonable clothing, and proper air and exercise. Given these things, they ought to as surely grow as seed that gets proper moisture and sunlight. As a rule children are fairly healthy when they are born. If they were not, they would never survive the fearful trials of their birth. Subjected to the same treatment which children receive, all the kittens and puppies which are born would never open their eyes.

Most children survive being weaned. After that most of them are poisoned by their mothers and their nurses. What is the first motive to look for? What are women most fond of? Of all things, sweets. Women simply love sweets, and, in their usual irrational way, they give children sweets. I have said "give their children sweets." Why, they simply stuff them with sweets! There is nothing they do not give them sweets with. They sweeten their bottles, they sweeten their bread, they give them sweets when they are good, they give them sweets when they are naughty! Indeed, I do not know when it is they do not give them sweets. I remember asking one of my own children what she had had for dinner. The prompt answer was "Pudding!" I was at first surprised at the apparent stupidity of an otherwise sharp child, and I said:

"Yes, you had pudding *after* dinner, but what did you have for *dinner?*"

"Oh! you mean the beginning?"

There you have it better than any grown person could put it. The child had simply been taught that pudding—which is simply an excuse for sugar—was dinner. The rest of her food was regarded as a sort of useless preliminary. The result is that most children die of sweets. Sweets simply ruin a healthy appetite, and are to children what drinking is to men. Next to their mothers, the chief murderers of children are their nurses. Nothing is so pernicious as the custom of nursery meals. It simply means that as the nurse and the children have, more or less, to eat the same meals, the nurse takes jolly good care the children have what she likes, rather than what is good for them. If she dislikes fish, for instance, she says the children cannot eat fish. The mother not knowing, and the children saying what they are told to say, they never have fish. It is the same with suet pudding or eggs, rice puddings, and all the rest of it. There is no good in saying this is not true, because it is human nature, and you can't go behind that. Then again, nurses love to feed children on what they themselves like. In their ignorant way, they think this is kind, and they are always feeding, even the youngest, children on meat. Far too much meat is given to children. They cannot digest it, more especially when their stomachs are destroyed by sweets and sips of beer and wine, and every other mess which women are never content unless baby has a taste of. As a rule, the diet of children would kill most men and women. From morning to night they are stuffed with food. Besides their regular meals, which are too big for their appetites, and not sufficiently frequent, they munch biscuits and cake and bread and butter, with layers of sugar or jam, from the time they get up till the time they go to bed, with the result that they have to be regularly physicked. Such violent remedies would kill a horse, and, indeed, it is akin to the system by which lightweight jockeys are killed.

Women think they can feed children by instinct. That's how they kill them. They also imagine that all children have the same digestions, and the result is, you find a whole nursery-full of children all eating the same food, and all subjected to the same treatment.

Could anything be more mad? Does it not stand to reason that, if some grown-up people, whose digestions, having survived the treatment of their youth, cannot eat the same food as other people, children require dieting too?

Some of the women I have spoken to on this subject have denied most things that others have admitted. They have said that men cannot manage their businesses, that men cannot manage their money, that men cannot manage their servants, and of all things, that they cannot manage women. It is only reasonable, therefore, to suppose that it will be denied that men can manage children. One thing is perfectly certain, and that is, that women do not. But I will ask those who will want to scratch my eyes out how they account for the fact that men do manage children, and manage them very well—more especially girls. A complete list of the large institutions managed by men would be impossible, but surely I may cite such large schools as those at Beddington, St. Anne's, and lastly, but not by any means least, the Masonic Girls School, which are not only managed, but magnificently managed, by men, many, if not most, of whom are bachelors, strange as it may seem.

I have already demonstrated that women have no idea how to properly dress children, and that their method of feeding them is something worse than foolish. If any other reason were wanted to prove that women cannot manage children, it could very easily be found. Children, everyone must admit, are mere creatures of impulse. The old proverb says, "Bend the twig as you would have it grow," and surely it must be acknowledged that children are, as a rule, abominably behaved. That each has a natural instinct peculiar to itself must also be admitted, but that children are naturally bad I do not at all think. None of their other inclinations are in any way developed; therefore, why should it be imagined that they are inherently naughty? As a matter of fact, they are not. They are largely imitative, of course, and if they saw good manners going on about them, they would as instinctively imitate good behaviour as they would bad. Everybody who has studied the question knows that they presume enormously, if they are allowed to do so; but in the first place, if they did not see bad manners, and, in the second place, were checked in a timely fashion, they would give pleasure to everyone.

It is quite the exception to find a child who is at all bearable. Their fathers and their mothers put up with them, of course; but where is the child who is at all fit to be brought down to see company, and who can behave at all decently in the presence of strangers? It may be natural to a child to resent a toy being taken from him, but it is not natural that a child should fling himself down on the hearthrug in paroxysms of rage on every available occasion. Children, as a rule, howl for everything; it is natural to them to cry when they are hurt, of course, but it is not natural that they should kick and plunge and bellow the whole house down because they are not allowed to break something of value. If they are taught—that is to say, allowed to

Children howl for everything.

believe—that they will get anything they want by crying for it, of course they will cry; but if they are taught that the one certain way of *not* getting anything is to cry for it, then crying is the very last thing they will resort to, for they are just as clever as monkeys. But women do not teach them this. As soon as the child cries for anything a woman will give it to him sooner than go through the ordeal of hearing him cry. A child crying is a painful sight, and the very best way to go about stopping it is to show him that crying will do him no good.

A great deal of the bad manners of children is due to their mothers, but not directly so. The people who spoil them most are the servants, and here, I think, the child has very just reason to complain of the treatment he receives. If you keep your children all day and all night, week in and week out, year after year, in the company of low-bred, vulgar, and disinterested persons like servants, how can you expect that your children will grow up and behave themselves like little gentlemen and ladies, and that they will be fit to come down to the drawing-room or the dining-room, or to behave themselves like Christians? It is not reasonable. Children ought to spend a very considerable portion of every day in the drawing-room with their mother, and should mix with her guests, and be taught to move about and not touch things, and not make themselves a nuisance to anyone. It is just as easy to teach a child to behave well as to behave badly. Of course, you must show the stronger will, but once you have established that, you can do anything with a child, and, believe me, it is the kindest thing to do. It must be distinctly understood, however, that I am no advocate for slapping or beating children in any way. It is absolutely unnecessary. The most unruly child will submit to a stronger will which prescribes slight punishments and sees them carried out. But if you once give way to a child, or go back on your word, you are making a rod for your own back, and your children, instead of becoming a comfort, grow up to be nothing short of little devils.

On the other hand, I do not at all maintain that you should never strike a child. There are some children who require it. They are very, very few, but there are some, as there are exceptions to everything. But there is one thing you should never do—you should never slap a child or correct him with your hand. There are two evils which result from this. The first is that no man or woman at all recognises how strong his or her hand is when brought into contact with the tiny frame of a child. You may hurt children very seriously, and much more than you ever know. The second reason for not correcting a child with your hand is that you may not hurt him at all, and this is just as bad as the other—in fact, rather worse. There is only one way in which you should beat a child. You must go out into your garden, and get the very smallest switch which you can find, and when the unruly young gentleman's clothes are taken off him, you should give him two or three, or four or five, sharp cuts where, as the French say, "Le dos change le nom." If you do this properly, you certainly will not permanently injure the child, and there is a very great chance that you may never have to repeat an operation which hurts you more than it does the child. But here again we have a proof of the absolute incapacity of a woman to manage children. A wife will contend with her husband that only women can manage children, but in the end she goes to her husband, and tells him that he must administer the corporal punishment, because she cannot bear to do it. This is not only bad for the child, but is grossly unfair to the man. It is a great shame that a father should be held up to a child as a bogey.

CHAPTER XI.

THE HOUSE DIRTY.

I WILL not confuse you, dear ladies, by telling you who it was who defined "dirt" as "matter out of place." It will be enough for your bird-like brains if you can remember the phrase, for one and all you dwell contentedly in dirt. If I were to leave this phrase unexplained, every single one of you would misinterpret it to mean that I thought you were not addicted to clean linen and the bath, or that your minds are debased by the witnessing of sights or the perusal of books "in which pure women may not look." I have my own ideas as to whether women, as a class, are better than men, but I am not arguing that point now, and so do not, as is too often your way, let us confuse the premises by going off into side issues. I hope you understand distinctly that when I say you dwell contentedly in dirt, I confine my remarks within the limits of the definition that "dirt is matter out of place."

In another chapter I have shown you that your basements are the real dust-holes of your houses. I think I have disposed of the contention of many that all the faults laid at your kitchen-doors are not the fault of your favourite bugbear, the servants, but that you are directly responsible for both servants and their faults.

It is now my intention to carry the indictment further by taking it into every nook and corner, and not only into every nook and corner, but into every open place and every closed space in what you love to call a woman's domain. I do not think even the strongest-minded and the most pugnacious of you will deny the partiality which your servants—women servants, mind you—have for sweeping dust and fluff into corners, under carpets, mats, and rugs, of disposing of burnt matches in fireplaces, of emptying dust-pans into baths, and sinks, and other places, and of leaving their brushes and brooms, their dusters, their blacklead pots, etc., etc., all over the house—in corners, under sofas, under (and even on) chairs, bureaux, on the stairs and landings, balanced on banisters, and indeed anywhere where they can temporarily dispose of them—to the entire disfigurement of the house when you come down in the morning.

This putting away of things in places "handy like" is a most deplorable system, but I cannot bring myself to blame the servants, for in it I see but a development of every woman's methods of what she is pleased to call "tidying up" or "making the place straight."

The clean and tidy little Japanese have practically no furniture at all in their houses. What they have is brought out when it is required for use, and when it has served its turn it is folded up and put away in its proper place. This is also their habit with decorations. When a guest is expected the walls are hung with pictures, when tea is served trays and stools are brought in, and you find the house decorated with bronzes, ivories, and flowers. If a guest were unexpectedly to return half an hour after his departure, he would find that the pictures had been rolled up and put away, and, indeed, that the gaily-decorated room was perfectly bare.

Now, I do not go so far as to say that you should strictly follow out these methods of those clean and tidy little people, though they are all instinctively imbued with perfect taste and are the greatest decorative artists the world has ever known. But I do say that you might go a long way in imitating them with great advantage to art and cleanliness. I am very fond of good furniture myself, as shall be demonstrated hereafter; but if a man of sense and taste were to go round his house and note and price all the hideous and superfluous articles that a woman strews round a house, he would be simply horrified. We have all a great deal too much furniture, even when it is of the very best, and our walls are over-crowded with everything which can be stood against them or hung upon them. To turn your walls into the semblance of a bric-à-brac shop or an exhibition of pictures is in the worst of taste, and to make your rooms into a sort of furniture warehouse, is to make your home uncomfortable at the expense of art. But when the pictures, vases, clocks, chandeliers, candlesticks, and other so-called chimney ornaments, are of the most crude manufacture and in the most detestable taste, a husband who respects himself and his wife ought to send away his family to the seaside, and go out and pawn all the "china' and glass, and Parian marble figures he can lay hands on, and lose the ticket and all

A bonfire in the back-yard.

memory of where he has disposed of them. He then should buy a box of matches, and having gone all over the house, and gathered together all the antimacassars, mats, bulrushes, art muslin, bamboo work, carved Swiss brackets, reed curtains, Birmingham Japanese fans and other eyesores and dust traps he can lay hands on, he should make a bonfire in his back-yard. Foolish men, who repeat the nonsense they hear, are in the habit of saying "It is easy to discern a feminine hand about a room.' *It is*, and if I had my way no woman should have a hand in such mischief as is found "for idle hands to do."

Women suffer from the delusion that they are neat by nature, and that it is their mission in life to "tidy up." Their way of indulging this itch is to stuff things away—anywhere out of sight. On these lines the magpie and the monkey are their masters. The real secret of tidiness is to leave things where they can be found by the persons who require them, and not to hide them away in blotters and presses and drawers; not to go into a man's study and to put all his papers indiscriminately into packages, or a receipted bill into an envelope which he is sure to destroy.

In a woman's eye every business paper is an unsightly object, which she considers it her duty to dispose of, and though she may hear the man who owns it cursing about the house,

she never has the grace of the jackdaw of Rheims to come forward and say what she has done with it. Indeed, she will deny with indignant innocence and tears that she ever touched his papers, and when, if haply it is discovered, he looks reproachful or smiles, she simply says, "Oh! is that what you are looking for? my dear, you should not leave such things about." Just as if he had no right to the use of a table or the corner of a chimney-piece in his own house.

Not only are women sublimely unreasonable in such matters, but their taste in the matter of decoration is most abominable.

I have accepted the definition that "dirt is matter out of place," and I have shown how important matters become dirt by being put by tidying-up hands "out of place." I have hinted at some of the ways a house may be made dirty and hideous by being filled up with every form of dust-collecting atrocity which can be manufactured. I will now turn my attention to how women can even misapply nature to this end. Few would deny that flowers are very beautiful things in their right place. When they are matter out of place, they become, of course, according to our definition, dirt. There are few of women's delusions so firmly rooted as that "nothing is so pretty about a house as a few flowers." There are not many women who can resist spending a large proportion of their house-keeping money on what they call a few fresh

flowers, on the pretext that the place would look so bare without them if anyone came to tea. Now, in the first place, the flowers are *not* fresh, and, even if they were, they have been the close associates of others which have probably spent the night under the bed of an East End lodging-house, inhaling every kind of dirt and poison it is possible to collect. In the second place, as they grow stale, they and the water they are placed in give off evil fumes. Besides, they are entirely out of place stuck on tables which are meant to be used; and what with the cutting of stalks, the staining of scissors, and the slopping of water in the initial stage, and the peril of their absurdly long and unstable glasses being upset and broken, they are about the most dangerous and most expensive folly that women waste their time over.

All that I have written here should go far to prove even to the prejudiced that women are untidy, and that, therefore, they permit or collect dirt about a house. This should be enough; but I feel that if I do not draw the contrast which I have always drawn, the feminine mind, which it is my mission to correct, might reply with their favourite "*tu quoque*"—which freely translated means, "you're another," and illustrates a woman's habit of arguing that two blacks make one white, two wrongs a right.

You, dear ladies, will no doubt say before

you have read any further: "Oh! I like that. Go into any husband's study and see how untidy it is." It is quite true that husbands' studies are not given up to nice tidy *art* muslin, bamboo, bulrushes, imitation bronzes,

and German "china" ornaments. They are filled with papers. Quite true! But papers are not necessarily more untidy than anything else, though you think so. What is the real reason why the papers are lying about? I will tell you. It is because, after years of experience, no man can trust you or your servants to touch his papers. Turn your eyes round his office next time you are there late. You will find all his letters are filed carefully, and his books are put away every night, and that he and his clerks can lay their hands on any paper at a moment's notice, while they know how everything which has gone away has been disposed of. That's what I call being tidy and being clear-minded.

CHAPTER XII.

THE HOUSE HIDEOUS.

IN the last chapter I inveighed against the furniture with which women lumber up their houses, and in my just indignation I went so far as to suggest that, after the Japanese fashion, we should have practically no furniture at all, and, really, though I meant to modify that statement in my present essay, I have a good mind to stick to my original plea. It is really extraordinary what slaves women are to custom, and the ordinary man is very much of the same unthinking way.

One of the most remarkable things in the world is the custom of keeping a dog—the most absolutely useless creature—for he does no work of any kind, and he is not good to eat. Yet man, who is supposed to be a thinking animal with his own thoughts to fall back upon, seems not to be able to exist unless he keeps a dog, which he feeds, buys a license for, redeems when it is stolen or strays, and pays continual fines for every time that it fights another dog, or mangles his neighbour's child. I suppose that one way and another, considering that many men keep many dogs, on an average every home in the United Kingdom pays at least £2 a year towards the support of dogs. The millions a year this represents it may amuse my readers to work out for themselves. The same applies to cats. I shall never forget seeing a very charming and benevolent lady of my acquaintance cut a plate of meat off her own joint and place it in the square for the cats to eat, while she stood by and saw that the hungry children, who could not catch sparrows or mice, did not steal it.

If I digress, it is but for the purpose of schooling you quietly into accepting the fact

that we are slaves to furniture as we are slaves to dogs and cats, for, really, the dog is not nearly so much "the friend of man" as man is the friend of dog. Of course, the real fact is that the dog is mentally the superior creature, and, being a philosopher—having settled in his own mind that work is all nonsense, that there is no such thing as riches, that all, even the most successful or brilliant, man ever gets out of the world is enough to eat and a bed to die in—the dog, like the woman, gives himself over to a man, displays a certain affection for him, and the vain, foolish fellow works hard, and keeps the dog in lazy luxury all his life. Men talk of hard work as "a dog's life." Was there ever such irony?

If man is the slave of dog, woman is the slave of furniture. If women only knew how much more graceful—and the only way is to appeal to their vanity—they would be reclining on the floor, they would never sit up on chairs or round a table. That this is fundamentally true is proved by the fact that they are never so happy as at a picnic, where there are no chairs and tables. I really believe that the craze for putting everything on something above the floor—by which I mean tables, sideboards, etc.—grew from the custom of sleeping in ugly, cumbersome, and dirt-collecting beds instead of on the floor. Of course, the reason why women do not sleep on the floor is because they are afraid of beetles, and mice, and other harmless things. Woman, therefore, having invented the bed, invented the table to stand by it,

and thus spread the habit of putting everything above the level of the floor.

Woman's original sin of being afraid of black beetles and mice costs man more than all the Royalty, armies, navies, pension lists, prisons, poverty, schooling, national debts, and wars of Europe.

I am sure I am not putting it too high when I say that the average cost of furniture per house is £200, and if the world would only agree not to cumber its rooms with beds and tables, sideboards, cabinets and chairs, our ground-rents would be about half what they are, and the over-crowding of our cities would come down proportionately.

But as women cannot be persuaded that black beetles are not poisonous serpents, and that mice are not man-eating tigers, it may be well to see how the furniture question, from the financial and hideous point of view, can be got over. Of course, half the difficulty of expense and ugliness would be done away with if all presses, cupboards, sideboards, seats, dressers, etc., which protrude into the rooms were let into the walls, thereby making charming recesses, and giving an opportunity for graceful arches.

But as most houses "are not built that way," some more practical suggestion is needed. To say that a sideboard, four feet by six, is required to support half a dozen tumblers, which ought to be kept in the pantry, and a cabinet of the same proportions is needed to hide a few pieces of music, is absurd. And so we see that a large proportion of our furniture is intended, not for use, but as ornament.

That most of the furniture which we find in middle-class houses is as bad in design and execution as it is in its lasting powers will be generally admitted.

Nearly every man's experience teaches him that when his or his friend's furniture is sold, it does not fetch a third of what it cost, and that fine old furniture purchased from a dealer fetches a high price. And yet, apparently, very few men and women learn the obvious lesson. Needless to say, the generality of men know little or nothing about the matter. To do them justice they generally admit as much, the result being that their wives, who think there is nothing to know, and who like spending money, undertake to procure "what is wanted."

They follow the same rule as they adopt in purchasing anything else. They go to a shop and ask the price of things which are as ugly as they are bad and expensive, and with these they fill their houses, and are

Something really cheap.

moved to tears when they eventually are sold and fetch nothing, as the popular phrase runs.

There are fifty-two weeks in the year, and not one of these passes that there are not some forty or fifty sales by auction in London alone. There is no doubt that a good deal of rubbish is sold at these sales; but I have attended hundreds in my time, and I do not think I am exaggerating when I say I do not remember ever having been to a sale at which there was not something really good and really cheap. Before making her house hideous for ever, of course a woman should learn something of furniture. It is a very easy and a very pleasant acquirement, and when once mastered, is a never-failing delight to herself and to all her friends, for it always makes conversation, and as long as a woman has something to talk about, she is happy; and men, who like her, think she is very well informed.

I could very easily write a dissertation on furniture, china, bronzes, and all the bric-à-brac which goes to make a house pleasant to live in. Such, however, is not my intention. Such information is plentiful, and I am quite sure nothing useful is to be learned therefrom. The best way is to potter about. I remember asking an old second-hand bookseller how he learned his business, and he frankly admitted that he picked up the greater portion of his knowledge from his customers. I have found by experience that this is the real truth. The fact is, nobody knows everything about anything; but anyone who knows anything will be only glad of a chance to show his knowledge to an appreciative listener, oddly enough, even if he is not a customer.

I well remember when I commenced buying nice things myself. Nobody could have been more supremely ignorant than I was. The reason, too, was an odd one. I had had a great reverse of fortune; we were very poor indeed, and the little new house into which we moved was almost as bare as the walls of a vault or a chapel. I said I should like to try and pick up a few nice things cheap, but everyone told me that those times had gone by; that people now know too much, and that I would only be "had." I did try, and I found, as usual, that what everyone said was wrong. Like everyone else who succeeds, I bought my experience in shillings, and made the world pay for it in pounds. The proof of the pudding is not in the eating, but in the digesting of it. I commenced very modestly by buying old Staffordshire figures, and of course I have been "had," but I have had my victories, and I can truthfully say that my collection of bric-à-brac, such as it is—and it would fetch a few thousands to-morrow—has not cost me one shilling.

But this is personal. The strange thing is that women who love to attend sales which are not "sales" at all in the proper acceptation of the term, and will willingly buy goods for 1s. 11¾d., which the day before they could have bought for 1s. 6d., will not attend auction rooms and buy really good furniture for a third of the money for which they can buy bad furniture in a shop.

Another reason for buying furniture when sold at auction is this. As a rule you have only the dealers to compete with, and it is always safe to outbid the dealers, who cannot afford, except in exceptional cases where they have a commission, to buy anything unless they can see a profit of 50 per cent. on it.

Then you offer him 5 per cent. on his bargain.

Another tip is, sometimes to let a dealer have something he is bidding against you for, and then to offer him 5 per cent. on his bargain. Unless it is a very good thing, which he can easily dispose of quickly for a large profit, he will generally take your offer, and you may reckon that it has cost you 45 per cent. less than if you bought it from the dealer when he had payed the expenses of taking it away to his shop. Having once done such a deal with you, he will probably not bid up against you on another occasion when you meet, and he may even pick his brains and those of his *confrères.*

CHAPTER XIII.

THE BEST REMEDY FOR ALL BLUNDERS.

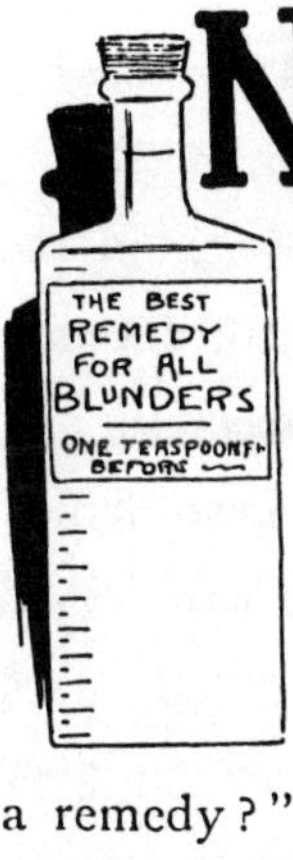

NO doubt at the end of every chapter my readers have put down this book with the ejaculation: "All this is very fine; but what does the man want?" Or, "It is very easy to find fault; but what's the good, unless the author is prepared to show us a remedy?" I ask for no kinder criticism, and if I only prevail on my fair readers to adopt my suggestion, I shall be content, for I have been "cruel only to be kind" to man and woman alike.

I commenced by saying "the house" was a branch of "the office," and that a wife should be a partner in the concern. That was my text, and I will be consistent and stick to it. I have far easier found the remedy than the faults. The remedy is quite simple. A business cannot be carried on unless accounts are kept. There is no good in denying this. It has been proved over and over again. It is easy to say "what's the good of keeping accounts of money that is spent? keeping accounts won't put the money back in the bank." That's right in theory, but it does not work out in practice. Keeping accounts *will* put money back in the bank. Dear ladies, this is business, and you don't understand business; but try it for a few years, and as a reward, leave me half the balance in your wills. My children will die rich if you do this.

You will not believe me when I say that, no matter how prosperous is the business of your husband, your father, or your lover, supposing any one of them were making a profit of £50 a day, and had done so for years, if he were to put that money in his pocket and not keep any accounts he would be bankrupt in a year. You don't believe it? You say it is only another of my paradoxes. Go to your husband, your father, or your lover, and ask—"What would happen to your business if you kept no accounts?" I should like to lay you a pair of gloves against the usual forfeit that they each say—"I should be bankrupt in a year," and every woman in England would give me a kiss on the same terms.

I suppose there are not many of my readers who will try, and I am sure there are very few who do try who will keep it up; but if they want to refute all my arguments, and make this book of no more value, they will expend one shilling on a simple little account-book, in which they will enter every penny they spend, and, most important of all, they will balance it up every week.

Household expenditure should be thus

regulated on business lines. The husband should enter into a working arrangement with his partner. A list of all expenses should be drawn up, and every week she should produce her book and ask for a cheque, not only to meet the average weekly expenses, but to include the rent, rates, taxes, wages, clothes, and school bills as they fall due.

It would be impossible in these pages to draw up a series of tables to fit all incomes and tastes. I have drawn up one, but I am sure some will say that 11s. 8d. is absurdly small for the butchers' book, and that 9s. is absurdly large for the fishmonger; there are people who think they are saving by having no fish and eating £1 0s. 8d. worth of butchers' meat. Some there are, too, who will say 6s. is absurdly little for washing, and others that it is too much. The explanation is that some "wash at home" and some do not. The items and amounts, however, do not matter at all. Arrange them all according to your own habits and incomes, but arrange them on these lines:

If your house rent is £45 a year, your weekly rent is 17s. 4d. That is arrived at by dividing £45 by 52, the number of weeks in the year. You will find it is a fraction under, but no husband with any sense will mind giving you the benefit of the fraction. Continue in the same way with every item of expenditure, and you will find the result will be something like the following:

	£	s.	d.
Rent, £45, ...	£0	17	3¾
Rates and Taxes, £12 11s. 8d., £1 2s. 2d.,	0	5	0½
Gas, £4, ...	0	1	6¼
Wages, £20, £20, ...	0	15	4
Charwoman, £6 10s.,...	0	2	6
Stamps and Telegrams,	0	2	6
Stationery, £3 3s., ...	0	1	4
Chemist, £4; Doctor, £5, ...	0	3	6
Cleaning Windows, 12s. 6d.; Sweeping Chimneys, 12s. 6d.; Repairs, £5, ...	0	2	6
Hardware and Linen, £5, ...	0	2	0
1 Child's Clothes, £5,	0	2	0
Wife's Clothes, £20,...	0	7	8½
	£3	13	3

Brought forward,		£3 13 3
Household Expenses :—		
14 lbs. Butchers' Meat at 10d.,	£0 11 8	
17½ qts. Milk at 4d. ; 24 Eggs, 1s. 3d.; 2½ lbs. Butter, 1s. 4d.,	0 11 8	
Bread and Flour,	0 2 2	
Fishmonger, ...	0 9 0	
Greengrocer, ...	0 3 3	
Grocer, ...	0 12 9	
Washing, ...	0 6 6	
Drink, ...	0 6 0	
Coal, ...	0 3 10	
Petty Cash, ...	0 4 6	
		£3 11 4
		£7 4 7

You will see from this that, if this fairly represents your expenditure, you are living at the rate of about £400 a year, for there are yet your husband's clothes, railway or omnibus fares, tobacco, etc., to be paid for, and only £24 1s. 8d. left with which to provide them. Still, if you would present him every week with a balance-sheet such as the following, I feel sure you would be able to lend him something to go on with from time to time :—

MODEL OF BALANCE-SHEET OF WEEK.

January 6th.

Received by Cheque, ...			£7	4	7

January 6th.

Butcher's Book, ...	£0	11	8			
Milk, ...	0	11	8			
Baker, ...	0	2	2			
Fishmonger and Poulterer, ...	0	9	0			
Greengrocer, ...	0	3	3			
Grocer,...	0	12	9			
Washing, ...	0	6	6			
Drink, ...	0	6	0			
Petty Cash, ...	0	4	6			
Coal, ...	0	3	10			
				£3	11	4
Average Rent, Rates, Taxes, Gas, Wages, Charring, Stamps, etc., Stationery, Doctor, Chemist, Clothes, Windows, Sweeping Chimneys, Repairs, Hardware, and Linen, as agreed per above list, ...				3	13	3
				£7	4	7

Having paid your household expenses of the week, amounting to £3 11s. 4d., you would have £3 13s. 3d. in your bank, and your following week's balance-sheet, provided your weekly books amounted to as much as last week, would read as follows :—

January 12th.

Balance in Bank, ...	£3	13	3			
Cheque received, ...	7	4	7			
				£10	17	10

January 12th.

Butcher's Book, ...	£0	11	8			
Milk, ...	0	11	8			
Baker, ...	0	11	8			
Fishmonger and Poulterer, ...	0	9	0			
Greengrocer, ...	0	3	3			
Grocer,...	0	12	9			
Washing, ...	0	6	6			
Drink, ...	0	6	0			
Petty Cash, ...	0	4	6			
Coal, ...	0	3	10			
				£3	11	4
Average Rent, etc., as agreed, ...				3	13	3
				7	4	7
Balance at Bank, ...				3	13	3
				£10	17	10

Having once more paid your household

expenses for the week, your balance at the bank would be £7 6s. 6d., and you would enter it on your next week's balance-sheet, being careful, of course, to see that the totals on each side balanced as before.

This may look very formidable at first sight, but it is really as simple as A B C ; and your husband would explain it to you, and straighten it up every week for you. As a matter of fact, you are sure to spend little sums which you will forget. I won't say that doesn't matter, but it doesn't matter much. The main thing is to keep some account, and the odd pence which you can't remember can always be put right by adjusting the "petty cash." Indeed, that is what the "petty cash" is for. If you will master this simple rule, you will have overcome the most serious of all the "Domestic Blunders of Women," and have attained, as I have,

THE END.

CORRESPONDENCE.

URUGUAYAN heartily endorses *A Mere Man's* arguments. "You are right," he says, "every time in your articles. I am glad to say that they don't touch my wife, who is wonderfully free from the mistakes you point out—though not as perfect as if she had been regularly trained to housekeeping as men are trained to business. Now do you not think that regular training schools should be started to teach housekeeping and domestic economy? They should be on a very strict business footing—

in fact, I think girls might go out as apprentices to restaurants and hotels. If they did so, then it would be an easier matter to get houses attended to by an outside gang of servants, *i.e.*, meals from the restaurant at the corner, housemaids and window cleaners in at regular hours, floor scrubbers, lamp cleaners, boot cleaners. etc., the whole job undertaken by a responsible firm for a single payment. Breakages and theft covered also. Girls who had had experience of hotel management would welcome such assistance.

"Our experience is that of the 'Housekeeper of Twenty Years,' that my wife knows too much for a bad servant to put up with. Consequently we have had perhaps a dozen changes a year, but as many come back to us again, and we often keep a good one some time—till they marry—it cannot be a bad place. We have, however, made a discovery, and find we can get a very superior class of servant, and any number of them at lower wages than an ordinary servant, and a far more intelligent class, but I must not give this away.

"But the trouble after all is that all the young men crowd round a pretty face and a smart frock, and don't ask for a certificate of competency before they marry—and therefore they must abide by the consequences of THEIR *unbusiness*-like conduct.

"You are right, too, about the children. My wife takes jolly good care of hers. We have been married ten years and never had the least disagreement, and she was one of the smart ones too."

. . . . . .

PEGGIE contributes the following amusing comment. "I take the liberty of sending you this old Scottish song in connection with the subject, with which you are dealing:—

JOHN GRUMLIE.

John Grumlie swore by the light o' the moon
And the green leaves on the tree,
That he could do more work in a day,
Than his wife could do in three.

His wife rose up in the morning,
  With cares and toils e'now,
'John Grumlie, bide at hame, John,
  An' I'll gae haud the plough.

'First ye maun dress your children fair,
  And put on them their gear;
And ye maun mind to turn the maut,
  Or else ye'll spoil the beer.
And ye maun reel the tweel, John,
  That I span yesterday,
And ye maun mind to ca' in the hens,
  Or they'll a' lay away.'

Oh, he did dress his children fair,
  And put on them their gear;
But he forgot to turn the maut,
  And so he spoiled the beer.
He merrily sang as he reel'd the tweel
  His wife span yesterday;
But he forgot to ca' in the hens,
  And the hens a' laid away.

The hawkit crummie let doon nae milk,
  He cream nor butter gat;
And a' gaed wrang, and nocht gaed richt,
  He danced wi' rage and grat.
Then up he ran to the head o' the knowe,
  Wi' mony a wave and shout,
She heard him, as she heard him not,
  And turned her stots about.

John Grumlie's wife cam hame at e'en,
  And lauched as she'd gae mad,
To see the house in siccan a plight,
  And John sae glum and sad.
Quoth he, 'I give up my housewife skep,
  I'll be nae mair gude-wife.'
'Indeed,' quo she, 'I'm weel content.
  Ye may keep it the rest o' your life.'

'Nae mair o' that,' quo' surly John,
  'I'll do as I've done before,'
Wi' that the gude-wife took up a stoot rung
  And John made off to the door.
'Stop, stop, gude-wife, I'll haud my tongue,
  I ken I'm sair to blame,
But henceforth I maun haud the plough,
  And ye maun bide at hame.'"

. . . . . .

N. B. is singularly appreciative, and says:—"I *almost* wrote to you after the inspired article on the 'Highly Respectable Person,' but the handle of the dresser drawer has settled it. You may be rather bitter, and at times somewhat unjustly sweeping in your remarks, but you certainly are the most wonderful man! I find it difficult to believe that you *are* one—but then no woman could write in quite such a trenchant style as yours. How do you find out all these little things that have been hidden deeply in woman's breast all these ages? I should like to know. *Do* tell me how you do it—it is, most of it, so wonderfully and fearfully true. But I do wish that after stating some glaring fault you would give us the remedy. You simply make us unhappy without cheering us up again. I really feel every week as if I had had a kind of mental shower-bath. I am not a particularly good housekeeper myself, but I am young (23), and have time to improve. I have a useful kind of husband, who is a great help to me in my various little difficulties. He is much impressed with your remarks *re* butchers and coal bills, and I believe intends to act on them, at any rate with regard to the latter. I am looking forward with the greatest interest to your article on children. If you can, tell me how to manage a painfully intelligent boy of three, who treats his mother with affectionate patronage, but never takes any notice of what she says.

"That is really a great difficulty of mine. He is *perfectly* good and obedient to his father, and equally fond of him, but I can't manage him at all; and the worst of it is the baby, another boy of eighteen months, begins to imitate him. I suppose boys are more difficult to manage than girls."

. . . . . .

A NON-IMPROVING PROPERTY begins an interesting letter by saying of "A Mere Man":—"I cannot feel quite sure whether he is writing a skit on domestic management, or whether he is writing it seriously. If the former, he is, I think, just a little too serious, if the latter, too sweeping. It is said a woman has no sense of humour; that being understood, I am going to take 'A Mere Man' seriously.

"He certainly states the case correctly as regards the many, but surely he will allow there is a very large exception that goes to prove this rule. English women labour under a great disadvantage in their domestic arrangements as compared with, say, the French and American, and, so far as I know to the contrary, many other countries. England as a whole is not happy without its absolute privacy in home life, its retail shopping, and consequently high prices, its washing days with its proverbial cold mutton; each little house has its own separate management, or as your 'Mere Man' would say its mismanagement. It is useless for him to compare it to his own or other men's businesses, the two things can never be parallel under present circumstances. His affairs are all worked on business lines and on a wholesale scale, where, as he says, estimates of different expenses can be obtained in all its branches. This could be done in households if we could bring ourselves to live as the French do; outside their homes chiefly, at cafés, restaurants, boarding-houses and hotels, where every thing is publicly arranged and catered for, and all is done on a business and wholesale system. As it is, with our craving for domestic privacy, we must put up with its attendant evils, with the exception of those comparatively few who are good managers and lucky in obtaining the co-operation of sensible servants and easy circumstances. And yet, with all my lack of humour, I still think 'A Mere Man' may be writing only a clever skit with a large amount of truth in it."

. . . . . .

GRANDMOTHER puts her points well:—
"As a woman of experience, I beg to offer a few observations. I have always thought and believed, and still do so, that domestic comfort is almost entirely in the hands of the wife; the husband can do little towards it, although he may observe that there is much to be done or altered. Nor can a husband so completely view a household as can his wife. If the wife is early, punctual, attends to domestic duties, so that the husband and father finds meals ready and well served, and

children and servants under proper control, he will in time, though perhaps slowly, learn to value and respect his home, and the wife will find in that her great reward; but if she fails in those duties, and she who ought to have been his guiding star is lost behind a cloud of idleness, frivolity, and perhaps extravagance, the husband is adrift, helpless, and finds comfort where he can.

"The tendency of the last thirty years, to train girls for the acquirement of knowledge, scientific, linguistic, mathematical, mechanical, and the utter neglect of domestic training, is bringing forth bitter fruit, and sowing at the same time the seed of future family misery. I can tell you of two nice girls of fourteen and sixteen, sent to a college daily, to the neglect of domestic interest; in about three years the younger was in her grave, overtaxed, both mentally and physically; in about five years the elder followed her. Neither of those girls could do needlework or follow any domestic pursuit. I can tell you of two more who said to their mothers, 'Oh take us home; we never see any of you.' Those mothers wisely did so. Where can a girl learn domestic duties if not in her own home? In Canada each girl takes a part in domestic work, and they prove good wives. Let mothers keep their daughters at home, denying them no reasonable educational advantages."

. . . . . .

A MERE WOMAN OF BRISTOL handles this subject sensibly. "I have read with very much interest, amusement, and, I must confess, a little anger, the letters of 'A Mere Man.' Your correspondent is not a new variety of man, by any means; in fact, he is quite a 'common or garden' sort, the 'man who knows,'—or thinks he does. We (apparently superfluous) women meet him frequently. While strongly protesting against 'A Mere Man's' unjustly sweeping condemnation of my sex, I am bound to admit, as I think will all women who have given the matter any thought, that he is justified in much of his complaint; but may a kindly providence preserve us from his remedy! He may prove in theory his superior fitness for the duties and responsibilities of 'home-keeper,' but I venture to say, not in practice.

"I feel very strongly on this subject, and have felt sad and indignant many times, as I have seen how very few women—comparatively speaking—seemed to realise their responsibilities and immense influence; but surely it is not because they are unfit and incapable of filling their place in the world. The real reason, it seems to me, is because women are not prepared for it. Every boy is prepared and trained for the business or profession he is to adopt; his education is conducted with that end in view, and he usually serves an apprenticeship under a master before he finally enters upon his career.

"In my opinion, the career of wife, mother,

and housekeeper is of more importance than any other, and to what business or profession is so little training and preparation given? At what college or school is a girl taught anything of importance, relating to the care of a home and children, the management and value of money? I believe a great deal more is being done than formerly, especially among the poor, but it is merely a drop in the ocean compared with what might be done, and though in many cases the home training is excellent, and, as a rule, a good housewife is the result, it is not so in the majority of cases.

"The poor mother has not the time, even if she has the ability, to teach her child housewifery. As soon as she leaves school she goes to help to keep another woman's house, without training, and disastrous is the result, as we who have to struggle with servants know; but that eternal grievance would be remedied if only a mistress understood what she required her servant to do.

"The average well-to-do and rich woman appears to think it quite unnecessary that her daughter should have a practical knowledge of nursing, cooking, and household management generally, in order to direct her servants, should she have a home of her own. I believe woman's place is by the *side* of man, *not* behind, and not in front, as some of my sisters appear to believe, and she should be given every educational advantage that man has, which, with her own special training, will make her far more fit to perform the duties of wife and mother than her uneducated sister.

"How can she manage the money entrusted to her with judgment and economy unless she has been taught the value of it? Does every man become a good business or professional man, and manage his affairs wisely and economically? What of the failures one too often meets, the men who are the 'hindmost' in the race for life and all it holds? It would be unfair to take such a man and hold him forth as a type of manhood, and say, man is not fit for the place in the world which he occupies; neither is it fair to take an incompetent woman and treat her as a representative of her sex. I cannot help thinking that 'A Mere Man's' domestic experiences must have been unusually unfortunate, to have given him such an unfair and distorted opinion of woman."

. . . . . .

E. J. J. writes with common sense. "Although agreeing with a great many of 'A Mere Man's' remarks, I cannot help seeing that in some respects he is rather unreasonable. How, for instance, can he expect his household expenses to decrease as his family grows up? As the children grow older, there is naturally an increase in the expenditure; there may no longer be school bills to pay, but there are others which more than take their place. A grown-up daughter requires far more amusement than a little girl in the schoolroom; she insists on being taken to all kinds of gaieties, and, greatest expense of all, she persuades her mother to entertain, and dinners, dances, and garden-parties are the result.

"All women are not good housekeepers, any more than all men are good men of business, but I feel sure that a house managed by a man would not, as a rule, be a success. Are bachelor establishments usually particularly well managed? Is not the unfortunate bachelor more often than not cheated right and left by his laundress and his housekeeper?

"Even a widower usually has an aunt or a sister to look after his house and children, and if he does try to get along by himself, in nine cases out of ten his children run wild, his servants are careless and idle, and his house dirty and untidy. Of course this miserable state of affairs also occurs when the wife and mother is indolent and undomesticated; but I, for my part, cannot think of a single case in which a man, left with a young family, has, alone and unaided, taken the reins of government into his hands, and produced a comfortable and well-organised household. 'A Mere Man' says, 'as regards children, men manage schools.' This is true enough, but men do not as a rule manage girls' schools; neither are little children sent to school, and, unfortunately, both girls and babies are to be found in most families. However, I have no doubt the men could get over this difficulty, and manage their children with the greatest ease, but I should be sorry for the children who were managed at home on the same principles as when at school."

. . . . . .

AN OLD DUTCH gives her opinions thus:—"Your accusations are too numerous and varied to deal with, but, as a wife and mistress of a house, I should like to say that my husband could enter his kitchen, late at night, as you suggest, without finding it the back slum of the house; neither would the drawers and cupboards be found to contain a heterogeneous mass of things. I have taken up the kitchen grievance in preference to others, because I consider that the state of things that exist in that department will generally prove what kind of a mistress is at its head. I think surely there are some of us who have a little respect for our husband's purse, and also for his comfort, though we may not get the credit of it, and I shall look forward, before you close your highly entertaining delineation of our characters, to the hope that you will discover we possess *some* good qualities as befit man's helpmeet, and that we are not altogether useless 'lumber' on the face of the earth."

. . . . . .

VASHTI speaks up for her sex as follows:—

"I presume you do not object to non-rancorous criticism, and consequently I am emboldened to take a brief on behalf of my fellow-labourers, and ask that a search-light may be thrown impartially over the whole question.

"To begin with, then, may I ask, with all deference, if you do not think that men are a little to blame for the state of affairs in their households?

"Would it not be reasonable to expect that when a man feels matrimonially inclined he should look out for use rather than ornament, *if* he wishes his household to be governed on the most economic principles? Yet how few do this! It strikes me very forcibly that during courtship outside attraction goes a long, long way in front of solid merit. I gather from your own papers that your wife was not chosen for her useful abilities. For what, then? I have no doubt for a pretty face and an engaging manner! Well then, sir, I do not think you ought to blame us for unbusiness-like ways in our houses, when by your own admission you choose the head officer of your household for the very qualities you would scout in choosing a clerk, and without one thought as to whether she was capable of filling the post you offered.

"Personally, I do not think it *is* reasonable to expect men to be entirely practical in a matter where love—real or so-called—is an important factor; but then I do not think they ought to upbraid their wives later on for the absence of qualities they were never asked to possess. I believe one of the first principles of political economy is, that demand creates supply, and we must hope that when fathers begin to realise that the young men of the future will expect their wives to be trained and proved housekeepers, they will take greater interest in the proper education of their daughters, instead of spending everything on their sons.

"To pass on to the question of servants, I much admire the theories you advance for their management, and think they would be excellent could they but be put into practice, but fear that unless a trades union for mistresses were formed it would be impossible to enforce them.

"Under the provisions of the Truck Act it

is illegal to impose fines on servants, or deduct for breakages from their wages, without an agreement, and suppose I were to try to make my servants sign any such document, I feel sure they would be wise enough to betake themselves to another situation where they could break with impunity.

"If you are serious in your desires for reform, I wish most earnestly you would act as a reformer and earn the gratitude of all mistresses by starting a trades union of this description. I should only be too pleased to give in my name as one of the first to join, and would bring many friends with me.

"I must tell you I am one of 'the few' who keep a stock-pot always going, and have soup in plenty all the year round, without buying any stock meat whatsoever. We also keep a pig, and consequently the objectionable tub, but I do not think much goes into it that ought not to do so.

"Regarding coal, it is certainly true we burn

more in winter than in summer, but not to an appalling amount; and considering that in summer we always have cold suppers instead of late dinner, I think the bills are pretty nearly as they ought to be. We buy flour and potatoes by the sack.

"In conclusion, I should like to add that although I have paid my bills regularly month by month for the eight years I have been married, I am positive I have not ruined my husband's credit, nor do I think it would be easy to do so, and I think in regard to that, you must have had small trades-people or clerks living in a large town in your mind, as I cannot think that regular payments could at all effect a professional man's credit.

. . . . . .

A. A. is at once complimentary and self-satisfied:—"I was delighted to read your article of this week on the management of children; your previous papers I have only read with amusement. They do not apply to us, as my husband would like to tell you; but *this* is a subject that deeply interests me. *Every word you say is true*, no language is strong enough in which to condemn the idiotic way of clothing children, which is considered by everybody a matter of course; it is marvellous to me that so many survive such treatment; but the discomfort the poor little things endure must be cruel. I have one child, a little girl of seven, who has been warmly and decently clad, according to your ideas and mine (and no one else's, it seems to me) from the time she was a few weeks old, and she has never had an illnesss in her life, and has been *entirely free* from the perpetual cold in the head from which most babies seem to suffer, and which is caused, I am sure, by such management, or rather *mis*-management as fills you with indignation.

"If you can arouse women to a sense of the proper way in which to bring up a child from its birth to the age of three or four years, you will accomplish one of the reforms of the century. I wish you every success in your crusade."

. . . . . .

A QUIET CRITIC writes as follows:—"I am much interested in 'The Blunders of Women,' being a woman who has blundered all her life! But I think, in common justice, Paterfamilias should go to the root of the matter, which is *Human Nature*, not *Woman Nature.* Man selects his mate through passion chiefly, and is naturally in a hurry—therefore he does not give himself time to select wisely. So, most men marry fools, or did—(the old order changeth—perhaps!) and fools breed other fools, and fools bring up their children foolishly, spoil their husbands, or worry them, or let their husbands ignore them. Ergo—blame Human Nature in *men* first, then eliminate it—if you can—and women will be wiser."

. . . . . .

AN ANGRY WIFE allows her feelings to run

away with her:—"I wish when you wrote that article about women that someone had strangled you.

"You have made my life a burden to me through my husband, what with your harness, and your bran-mash, etc., and your mutton, chops, and so on. There are no words in the English language bad enough that I could throw at you. Please close your series at once as they won't do any good at all, and are only making strife in once peaceful homes.

"P.S.—I feel so mad I could chew his skin."

. . . . . .

HOMO speaks out and says:—"'A Mere Man' is rather over-reaching himself. At first there was a large undercurrent of truth in his letters; lately, however, he seems to me that he is greatly exaggerating the 'Blunders.'

"I am a married man—and have been so a long time—I never saw my kitchen in the state he mentions. I have been in the kitchens of many other houses, and have never seen the mess there either.

"With regard to the 'servant question,' it is easy to take the stand he does respecting the management—but you cannot do with them as you would with your clerks. With clerks the supply is greater than the demand — with servants the demand greater than the supply—and the result is the servant has the whip hand. Still there is truth in what he says—a good mistress makes a good servant. My wife has no trouble to speak of with hers, and she keeps them a long time —one great secret being, from what I can see—always to be 'firm, friendly, but *never* familiar.'

"Well, our mutual friend may be able to manage his household affairs better than his wife, but I am jolly well sure I could not—nor could the bulk of my friends manage theirs as well as their better halves. I am quite certain there is not an atom of waste in any single way in this house, and were it not for my wife I should be a poorer man to-day than I am.

"One point has struck me, and it must have struck others.

"Of necessity 'Mere Man' has formed his original impressions from his own home—for he could not have obtained them from outside sources, since men as a rule are not fond of airing such grievances—is he not, then, giving himself away, and coming to the conclusion that all homes are as badly managed as his own?

"One more point. Economy to a certain extent is all very well, but do you think that every man wants to run his home upon the same lines as his business? Is there not enough scheming, sweating, haggling, etc., in the average man's daily life to satisfy him? To me it is positive relief to be able to pay, say, my grocer a halfpenny a pound more for bacon, than necessary; it doesn't hurt me, and may mean to him just the difference between loss and profit. This everlasting competition is wearing men's lives out in business—why force it into private life if not absolutely necessary?"

. . . . . .

A MATTER-OF-FACT MAN finds much excuse for "women's blunders" and for the "shortcomings of servants":—"I feel," he writes, "that your criticisms are fully justified; but, at the same time, it is in a large number of cases more the misfortune than the fault of women that they are deficient in the art of management. Their weak point is the want of training for the position of household manager, wife, and mother.

"For any other occupation or position in life an apprenticeship, or course of training, has to be gone through; but any and every young woman thinks nothing of undertaking the management of a house and the responsibilities of wife and mother, even though unable to cook an omelet or to sew a button on a shirt.

"How many thousands of young women are there amongst us growing up to marriageable age without any training or guidance in the art and technicalities of household management? This is mainly their mother's fault, but the father also has his share of the responsibility.

"It is only by great good luck nowadays that a young fellow can secure a partner for life who, in addition to the ordinary education of her class, has even moderate skill in the details of domestic duties. It is very sad, and leads to much mischief and unhappiness, this ignorance of theirs.

"As for the servant question, what can be expected of them when one thinks of the examples of incompetence, and too often of frivolity and indolence, that are daily before their eyes? Where are they to learn method, system, and attention to details?"

. . . . . .

It is the opinion of AN EXCEPTIONAL WOMAN that "A Mere Man" would do a great deal of good by his letters if women could only find it in their hearts to be less prejudiced and a little broader-minded with regard to a man's judicious interference in domestic matters.

"If women," she says, " would look at housekeeping in a more business-like way, I feel sure that their husbands, themselves, and their children would benefit greatly thereby. It stands to reason that a successful man of business must know something of what he is about, and that such a man would not interfere in his wife's domestic arrangements without good cause, so that if the wife of such a man would listen patiently, without prejudice, she must obtain *some* advantage from his advice. But, as a rule, women will not listen, or, if they do so, with their mind made up beforehand that he knows nothing, and that his advice is, in consequence, unworthy.

" But is this, after all, all a woman's fault? I think a woman is treated much more unfairly than a man. In her girlhood she is taught, besides her ordinary education, which she shares with her brother, to play the piano, to do a little painting, and drawing, and sewing, and then she is considered as an accomplished woman, fit to take the responsibilities of a wife and housekeeper, the business in life of the majority of women.

"But her brother is only allowed one or two of these accomplishments by way of recreation. He is put in his father's office, he is apprenticed to his business, and taught it thoroughly from the first grade upwards. Who would ever thrust a young man into a post as manager of a business without his first having had a training for it, and expect him to manage it in a proper manner without having anyone to show or guide him. But this is what is thrust upon women, and then they are blamed for their blunders.

"If fathers insisted upon their daughters being taught properly, and, like their brothers, apprenticed in their own particular line of life, *their* husbands and children would feel the benefit of their education, and this would tend to enlarge and broaden the minds of the women themselves, which are, without doubt, much biased and crippled in this respect at present."

. . . . . .

OLD BUFFER writes:—"Dear 'Mere Man,'—All praise to you for your outspoken papers.

"If anything is required to clinch your remarks on the insane 'short-coating,' the following figures from the tables of mortality should do it:—

LONDON MORTALITY.

Age.	Number living.	Decrement of death in the next year.
Birth	10·000	3·191
1 year	6·809	1·235
2 "	5·574	538
3 "	5·036	360
4 "	4·676	243

"Thus, in the first year, 32 per cent.; in the first two years, 44 per cent.; and the first three years, 50 per cent. of the children born die, many of them, no doubt, from the undue exposure of their tender little bodies.

"Peg away, my dear sir, peg away!"

. . . . .

SEASIDE seems pleased. She says:—"I find the articles by 'A Mere Man' most useful and instructive, and hope they will enlighten silly women to obtain more sense, and be able to make better use of money, and if married, study home and husband better than they have done. Badly-trained mistresses are the *real cause* of bad servants. Our great-grandmothers (who had one or two silk dresses, and quite content to make these last for years) taught young girls cooking, housework, needlework, and kept these girls in their service for years, and the mistresses were loved and honoured for their teaching; but in these days, how the women have degenerated. Study fashion and go about with exaggerated clothes, and look worse than the poor Hottentot. How is it possible to obtain good working-girls when they have such a bad example?

"I am thankful that your remarks do not touch me. My husband thinks my cooking and house management perfect, and I never trouble him with domestic details, but spend his money with care and foresight. I know how hard he has to work for it. Thrifty ways are often thought mean ways, but only the ignorant think that, for a woman well-trained, who understands the chemistry of the kitchen, can afford to be more generous than her wealthy sisters, who fling away and waste the good substance our Maker provides."

. . . . . .

A HOUSEKEEPER gives her opinions thus:—"I read your article on the management of servants with great interest, and seeing that you request your lady readers to give you their ideas on the subject, will try and give you mine.

"You say 'a mistress is to blame for a bad

servant, and that it is owing to the lazy way in which women do their work that all servants are more or less amateurs.' I fancy a good deal of the trouble lies with young married women, who have little or no experience in housekeeping, engaging young servants as inexperienced as themselves. Therefore I think every girl who contemplates taking on the responsibility of housekeeping should have a thorough knowledge, both of the cost of the materials, and the way in which the work is done; if she had this, she could correct her servant properly, and also see that the materials were used to the best advantage; for, as everyone knows, an experienced worker does not waste.

"It does not degrade any woman to work, and it would give a greater sympathy between mistress and servant if the former knew what it was to feel tired.

"Next you say: 'In every business in the world which is managed by men, and novices are employed, they are taken as apprentices and taught their trade.' I do not see how this applies to servants and mistresses. Regarding the apprentice and his employer, this is as it should be; the employee has to pay down a sum to be taught his trade, or gives his time as an equivalent. No business man would take a novice to waste his time and spoil his materials with no compensation, whereas no servant would give time, or could afford to pay to be taught her duties; neither are there many mistresses, who, while paying her, would care for the task of teaching, even should she prove a docile pupil.

"I do not agree with you when you say, 'All women are lazy, and only those have succeeded who have been thrown upon their own resources.'

"Where a woman has a healthy interest in life and her fellow-beings, I am sure she is the reverse.

"There are women, 'and men also,' who seem to take no interest in anything outside themselves, and therefore naturally let things drift, while they become both inanimate and selfish. You also say, 'As long as men are content to be merely backers, and people who provide the money to keep up a fad which they call "home," so long will women let things drift, without making the home a good investment.' Of course, when a' man is a mere backer, and takes no deeper interest in the home than providing the money to keep it up, I can understand the woman taking no interest either; but when it is mutual, it is a pleasure to both, and becomes a pride to the woman, and a place of rest to the man, where he can forget his business worries.

"I rather fancy that it's not such a bad investment after all, at any rate in a case where the husband and wife are old-fashioned enough to care for each other.

"I quite agree with your proposal of a written agreement, binding both mistress and servant, and also that each servant should be made responsible in a form for the things under her charge. That would of course do away with the bother of a new servant coming and complaining that everything was broken. Next as to the work being put on the statement, in the case of a cook or housemaid, it would be comparatively easy to portion out the work to certain days; but in the case of a general or only servant, whose duties are more varied, it would prove more difficult, and could only be done where the mistress managed her house in a systematic way. In this, far more rests with the mistress than the maid. What you say regarding the wages and characters of servants is quite right and fair, and I feel sure that by giving a servant the chance to redeem her fault, and making it worth her while to do so, you are far more likely to gain her confidence and respect, in doing which you turn an indifferent servant into a good one."

. . . . . .

A MERE GIRL writes with considerable ability and point. She says:—"Your letters on our domestic blunders have amused, interested, and occasionally made me very angry. I quite agree with you that we girls are badly educated in domestic matters, and have occasionally to buy our experiences. But it is not altogether our fault. Until eighteen or nineteen we are kept busy passing exams., in order to fit us for work in case of depreciation of property, and then—if there be no mother—paterfamilias deserts his club, and settles down, while his daughter is supposed perfectly capable of 'running' a house without assistance. I speak from personal experience.

"I disagree with you about servants. Irish mistresses are perhaps more lucky or more human; they take an interest in their maids, and even when they have to find fault, do so with a laugh. The maids don't get so much animal food (I mean beef and mutton), and are much worse housed as a rule than English servants; but I think you will find Irish mistresses, or at least 70 per cent. of them, keep their maids until they either marry, or are borne off by some brother or sister to America. O America, how we Irish mistresses hate you! Englishwomen (in Ireland) act as though maids were of a different breed, not of the same flesh as themselves, when they find fault; they pull a long face and nag, and if there be an English servant in the household, they listen to all the tales she chooses to carry. Then they are sometimes given to worry servants about their religion, which I consider simply an impertinence on their part. Perhaps I have been exceptionally lucky, but we live in Dublin, and six months in the country—my country cookie won't leave here, and the Dublin one won't leave Dublin. Still, though these changes have continued for six years, I have the same cooks, both good ones, and, with the exception of one parlourmaid who married, exactly the same staff as I had six months after I started keeping house. Each cook takes 'job' work while I am away, and—though we only give £18 a year—always comes back gladly.

"I do approve of weekly bills; they keep a decided check on the expenditure. I have to show them every week to my father, which is annoying—as if he is 'low' about any new Land Act, he carps at every item; whereas, if he gave me £25 a month, I would undertake to buy coals, gas, whisky, liquor (except champagne), pay the maids and boy their wages, and 'run' the house with the exception of rent and taxes on that sum—and do it very comfortably too. That would only come to £300 a year; yet all the summer we have visitors, and for a good part of the winter.

"Of course, fish, vegetables, and fowls are much cheaper in Ireland; but then, on the other hand, we are usually at the mercy of a local butcher and grocer, the only ones in the neighbourhood, whom you must deal with, or get things from town, when the cost of the carriage makes the expenses equal. I am afraid if I attempted to bargain with our butcher here in the way your ideal woman does, he might yield to me, but he would send me what fat and bone he pleased, with the joints; whereas now, I either stand over him when he cuts them, or return them if they are not as I please. I speak by the card in this matter, as the coastguard officer's wife near here gets her meat at contract price (it is a little irregular on her part), and is always complaining of the marvellous amount of waste meat that is sent in.

"We are all fond of amusement, and like to keep plenty of money for gadding, therefore I look at things in a business-like manner, so I can tell you exactly almost what each guest costs. A woman makes a difference of 2s. 6d. to 3s. a week, mostly in vegetables and fruit, and a man 7s. 6d. to 10s. if he be a moderate drinker. If he be above average in that line, it comes to a little more. I can manage with three guests on my £25 a month, each guest staying the month, but it is a bit of a pinch. As we are only four in family, each additional person is felt; but in a large family it should make little or no difference, except in the wine bills. We give both here and in Dublin small dinners and picnics, and theatre parties, and people are always dropping in from the links. I must confess, dear 'Mere Man,' I don't mind one man to dinner unexpectedly, but neither cookie nor I can do ourselves justice when three hungry men descend on the family just half an hour before dinner with appetites whetted by two rounds of golf.

"In this household we young ones have an income of £500 a year. We pay half the household expenses, and my father the other half, therefore it is to our profit to keep down expenses if we want a little gad to London and Paris occasionally, and I like part of May and June over your side immensely.

"I *am* so sorry for you if your wife be such a bad manager; but don't you think if you gave her a regular sum a month, she would do better and make you more 'comfy'? And I think you must have exaggerated the breakages in your house 'just a wee,' as they say here. My estimate covers all breakages and doctor's bills, too; and everything must be entered in my household book for father. If he has been playing golf—well, he never grumbles, but if not—oh! How I dread 'Black Monday'! Aren't you a little bit like that too—eh? And it *is* so hard for your wife, she can't swear or show temper. Sometimes I do want someone to say 'Damn!' so badly for me."

. . . . . .

A FRIENDLY CRITIC says:—"Like many other women readers, I have been following your course of articles with great interest. Though unwilling to say so, I must admit that you have put your finger on many sore spots in our domestic life and management. But you appear to me to lay to our door sins for which we are not responsible. You say 'the plague of London hardly equalled the infant mortality of London alone.' The same might probably be said of any large city, and as women are the caretakers of the children of these cities, you argue that they are to blame for the high infant death-rate.

"Is it not a fact that the large death-rates of all our cities are produced by deaths amongst the children of the poor? Is it not also a fact that amongst the poor the mother of the family goes out to daily work of some kind or other, and is in many cases the sole breadwinner for her family? She may do the best she can to provide someone to look after her children in her absence, but what proper supervision can there be in such cases?

"Again, are not many deaths directly or indirectly due to starvation? Is the unfortunate mother of the family to blame when the earnings, scanty at the best—which ought to provide food for the children—are spent in drink, or when bad times come, and there are no earnings at all? Again, I do not at all agree with you that nearly all children are born healthy. Very many come into the world handicapped by hereditary disease.

"When you speak of institutions for girls admirably managed by men, do you mean to say that in such institutions there is no female superintendent, or that in every detail the working of that institution is carried on by men? To go back to the subject of infant mortality, it would be interesting to find out what proportion the infant death-rate bears to the remaining death-rate amongst the classes where the mother of the family is not compelled by sheer necessity to be wholly or in part the breadwinner. If you could prove that the infant mortality in these classes is out of proportion to the entire death-rate of those classes, you would have done much towards establishing your case against us."

. . . . . .

MATERFAMILIAS says:—"I would like to say a few things in reply to 'A Mere Man's' chapters on 'The Domestic Blunders of Women.'

"He complains of the expense of keeping up his house increasing instead of decreasing. It is only natural that it should increase. Supposing that a man after marrying becomes the father of a family, as 'A Mere Man' has done, there being the additional expense of providing for the family. A nurse or two nurses, food and clothing for the child or children must be paid for. Then when the children grow older, though the nurses can be dispensed with, there are school fees to be paid, and as the daughters (or sons) grow older, they take up extra subjects, which are paid for separately from the school fees.

"The best way for 'A Mere Man' to find out how badly (or how well) he can manage a house, is, that he should himself try some practical housekeeping.

"Let me ask 'A Mere Man' to try buying beef and mutton for his household. Does he know how much he would require to buy? Can he instruct the cook how to cook any new dishes which may come into fashion? And lastly, can he sew or darn stockings, or does he think that, with practice, he might do as well as a woman? I, for my part, think he could not.

"He says in one of his chapters, 'I have noticed that they (*i.e.*, women) will read and believe anything that appears in a newspaper.' Print your letter in a newspaper and see how many women believe it all, 'Mere Man.'

"He states that he has studied 'advice to women about housekeeping, and that it is clear that those giving the "advice," have no houses, husbands, or families to look after,' that is, that they have no experience. Let me ask 'A Mere Man' what experience has he?

"He also states that 'A woman always regards her management of a house as perfect.'

Again let me ask if a man does not consider his management of an office as perfect, and what is more, better than the management of any other man?

"Lastly, I would like to state that it is the opinion of the general public that the food supplied at restaurants and such places is very much inferior to that supplied in private houses."

. . . . . .

MATERFAMILIAS writes much shrewd common sense, and says, in her frank, outspoken reply:—"I expected a much more convincing attack, as it is easy to find fault even with the best regulated households—or offices—and we poor women are far from pretending, for one moment, that a great deal of what we do could not be better done. But our mentor, in this instance, after many preparatory assertions as to what he was going to do, seems to me to have accomplished very little; and I think any unprejudiced person who has read the papers would conclude they had been indicted under the well-known advice, 'No case, abuse the plaintiff's attorney!' This 'Mere Man' appears to have very well carried out, for the greater part of his first paper is occupied with sentences like these—'I do not know any detail of domestic life that I, or any other man, could not manage better than women do'; or, 'There should be nothing simpler in the world than to manage a house, a few servants, and a few children on a regular income'; or, 'I propose to . . . show why women fail in the simplest details of administration,' and so on, and so on. In fact, Chapter I. is altogether taken up with complaints, backed by 'I will show you how to do it better.'

"In Chapter II. we are treated to some practical details, and these will be dealt with later on; but in Chapter III. there is a return to the above tactics, and expressions like 'the absolute incapacity of women,' that they have 'no capabilities for saving money,' and have 'no idea of its value,' that they 'are really as much afraid of it as a loaded pistol,' and that they 'are not only conniving at the robbery of their husbands, but are ruining his credit,' run riot through its pages; and, to crown the whole, we are treated to perhaps the most fantastic financial proposal for the payment of household bills that it has ever been my lot to encounter; but of this more anon.

"In the first place I maintain that the real point has been shirked and glossed over by 'A Mere Man' in his few opening remarks, and that a fictitious value has been given to this question of household expenses which it does not deserve, praise not being accorded where praise is due.

"We are told he married his wife because he loved her, he has worked hard for her, and, in comparison with his office, what has he got for it? what are his assets? Now, it appears to me that an office is run for one thing, and for one thing only, and that is to make money; but the home is created for a very different reason. It is to provide a companion in his joy and his sorrows, and for the man a loving companion, who endeavours to sustain him in his troubles, and who tends and cares for him in his times of sickness. A *mother* for his children—one who will educate them in the way they should walk, teach them to fear God, honour their father and mother, and become good and upright men and women.

"I take it that it is infinitely more necessary that a woman should be a good wife and mother than that she should be somewhat sharper at reducing expenses than a professional housekeeper. 'A Mere Man' seems to purposely miss these points. He talks of the fictitious value of love; but can love be valued? I think not.

"Again, he refers to his wife as 'not an improving property,' which is as heartless as it is unfair, because there is no doubt that she is at least as an improving a property as he is himself. However, having given the proper prominence to women's true vocations, against the smallest one of superior housekeeping advocated by 'A Mere Man,' I will now go on to discuss his assertions, and I think it will be easily proved that a house managed upon the lines he suggests would be worse than one run upon any ordinary plan.

"He opens in Chapter II. by the assertion that 'nearly all we earn is spent on our homes and *the luxury of our women folk*.' The last part of the sentence must be met by a flat denial. Does anyone, even a 'mere man,' believe within his innermost heart that a woman spends as much on her luxuries as he does? What about those 70s. a hundred cigars, and that 60s. a dozen port, which is carefully kept for his own consumption? not to mention those luncheons to business friends, at which champagne and liquors play such a prominent part.

"But we will not press the point; let us on to some practical 'suggestions.' Even here, in this paper of 'proof,' they are difficult to find; but, as far as I can discover, the chief one is that a discount should be insisted upon from our bakers, butchers, and greengrocers. The passing remark that a woman does not know what her beef and mutton costs in the field is too absurd for serious consideration. Does a man know what his cigars cost in the leaf, or his wines in the grape? And would it be any good if he did?"

. . . . . .

A LANCASHIRE WOMAN says:—"I am a middle-class woman, and since my marriage I have lived in three different counties, the people in each representing very different types of character, and very rarely have I met with a woman of the thriftless character which 'A Mere Man' ascribes to the whole of my sex.

"I know a great many women whose purses vary in length, but all of them make a point of not only ordering but choosing their meat; and most of them consider, from a health point of view, that vegetables are too important an item to be discarded for the sake of saving an odd halfpenny.

"If 'A Mere Man' pays fourteenpence a pound for chops in London, I should not like to live there. But does he know the price? or is it guess work? I pay elevenpence for the best quality.

"All the women I know check the grocer's and baker's bills very closely. I buy my bread by the stone, and know how many loaves go to it. I can tell 'A Mere Man' of more than one man who owes his success to his wife's thrifty habits at the commencement of their married life.

"With regard to buying coal by contract, I wonder how many middle-class husbands would allow their wives to pay for twenty tons of coal in advance? Most women are satisfied to pay cash on delivery.

"'A Mere Man' thinks it very easy to manage a few servants and a few children. He quotes how men manage clubs, restaurants, schools, etc., but does Paterfamilias know that both maid-servants and children stand more in awe of a man than a woman?

"Women give too much time to afternoon teas and idle gossip, but they are not thriftless, neither will they see the husband's or father's money wasted."

. . . . . .

ONLY A WOMAN says:—"'A Mere Man' has dipped his pen in gall. From the bitterness of his heart he speaketh. One even ventures to doubt his affections for that poor lady who in her declining years he wittily calls 'not an improving property.' He mentions restaurants and schools as a proof that men can manage house, servants, children, if they turn their minds to it. We can choose our restaurants and schools, and can change them if we like, so this does not prove much.

"Marriage is truly a leap in the dark, and the writer of 'The Domestic Blunders of Women' has evidently not been happy in his venture. One cannot help pitying his womankind and him. However, we await his utterances in a meek and quiet spirit, and hope that in the inevitable storm in a tea-cup which must follow, there will be some flashes of truth that may help us women in our rather thankless task of managing, as we best can, house, servants, and children."

. . . . . .

YORKSHIRE WOMAN takes a somewhat logical tone:—"Conscience tells me there is some—perhaps much—truth in your papers on the 'Domestic Blunders of Women,' but I should like to draw attention to a point which I think you, and men generally, overlook. Character—even a woman's—is to some extent consistent, and the qualities which men usually admire in a woman are, I think, not those which are correlative with business acumen. There are women who can make a bargain with trades-people or others with the astuteness of a business man; but it is scarcely likely that such a one will have the grace, *naïveté*, and general winsomeness which a man really reckons among the chief charms of woman.

"In choosing a wife, a man usually desires a womanly woman, and avoids the 'strong-minded,'—so-called—of the sex. He must be prepared therefore to find her wanting in some of the qualities which he would require in a partner of his own sex. At the same time, he may justly expect her to be a reasoning and reasonable being, and able to enter into his views on pecuniary and other matters with intelligence.

"But the training must commence before marriage, and it is very desirable that from first leaving school, a girl should have an allowance, and be shown, if she does not know, how to keep a simple cash account. It should be clearly understood this allowance must not be exceeded, or it will do harm instead of good. I think her father may well require to see her account quarterly, for the first year or two at least, to be sure it is being correctly kept. This forms a basis of accuracy which will be useful in the larger field of housekeeping.

"Given an average woman, I think it an excellent plan for the wife to receive a weekly allowance to cover all expenses connected with housekeeping, except perhaps coals and servants' wages. It saves all 'bickering' between the two. It should be large enough to cover needful replenishment of household linen and utensils, which may be done gradually with a little management. This plan seems to necessitate the payment of ready money, which you disparage; but I think if the stipulated allowance were adhered to, you would find the method a great saving, even though some interest on the money were lost. This, I think, can be obviated in part, by dealing, as far as possible, at ready money stores, where equal goods are supplied at lower prices."

. . . . . .

R. M. C. says:—"You speak about servants being terrified to give notice to leave their situations. I have found most of them cannot even be slightly and kindly reprimanded for the slightest mistake without replying, 'Then if I don't suit, I had better go at once.' I am as kind and considerate as possible (my record showing that I have kept my servants many years), but I do not think they take into consideration the advantages of good food and a good home, for they generally tell you 'they can soon get a better one and more money.'

"Especially during the last six years I have found this tone adopted by servants, who also seem to look upon the poor unfortunate 'she' as their natural enemy. One of my servants informed me 'that her former mistress was a "she-devil,"' while I knew she was a most kind and indulgent creature, never refusing her servants a favour if she could help it.

"I quite agree with your next remark

'that we are greatly indebted to our servants for most of the comforts of home,' but it *must be good* servants, willing and good-tempered, and who like and take interest in the family they live with; bright and happy-looking servants naturally make the mistress the same, and so when Paterfamilias returns, 'All is Peace.'

"I am sadly afraid the fault lies with the mothers of the girls, who, when they first go into a situation, hardly know how to wash a cup or glass properly. Perhaps, after all, the mothers are not so much to be blamed, as they cannot train their girls to be good servants, while the School Boards are training them to grow up *useless* young women.

"One more word, and that is about the mistresses. There are men who delight in speaking of their wives as chums, liking them to boat and bicycle with them. How on earth can they manage a house with children and servants properly when they are away from it half the time? No man succeeds in his business (no matter how good and trustworthy his assistants may be) unless he is on the spot. The same rule should apply to mistresses. I hope these articles will not increase the servants' self-importance—they think quite enough of themselves as it is, and I am afraid the poor mistresses will have to put up with more than ever.

"I think these articles ought to do some good to those whom 'the cap fits.'"

. . . . . .

SYBIL stands up bravely for her sex. First:—"I admit that in a sort of whimsical way 'A Mere Man' has cause for at least *some* of his complaints. There are undoubtedly some very badly-managed homes, and there are many women who have no financial capacity at all; but it is not always—or even generally—the women who cannot keep accounts whose homes are uncomfortable, nor the mathematical women whose households are ideal. I have often thought that men—especially business-men—are apt to carry business principles too far. Why should a home be burdened with the sordid consideration of whether every transaction with every tradesman or every workman has resulted in the largest possible advantage to oneself and the smallest to him? That appears to be the soul of *business*, but it does not seem very ennobling.

"In my experience—nearly ten years of married life—I have found that butchers are, in a sense, honest. That is, if I go and choose or order a certain joint I get it—I know the price of each joint—and if I order the best I pay for the best. If I do *not* get the best I complain, but seldom have to complain twice. With regard to 'beating down' a tradesman, I never do that; but I know women who do, and I also know that they gain nothing by it.

"The 'Mere Man,' however, gives no weight to the possibility of women's lives containing more intellectual duties than haggling over *chops*. If it were not so, it would indeed be asked by womenkind, 'Is life worth living?' For my part, I should consider it absolute waste of time to call personally at every shop each time the necessary household purchases had to be made, although my home is 'buried' in the country, where the eternal 'calling for orders' is unknown, and considerable forethought has to be exercised in order to keep up the household stock of every kind.

"I think the 'Mere Man' exaggerates the condescension of man in marrying woman. After all, a man marries of his own freewill, and he *should* have the sense to realise—with his vaunted business capacity—that his household expenses will *increase* and not decrease year by year. I believe most men vaguely fancy that when they furnish a house—say on their marriage—they have bought all they will require in that house for the rest of their natural life; and then when, in a few years, some more saucepans have to be invested in, they feel grieved, and think that someone has been very much to blame. Saucepans will not last many years, however well they are treated, nor will 'children's stockings,' alas! Many weary mothers can testify to that.

"Men have their own business worries—why should they add to them the infinitely more worrying worries of domestic economy? Most women bear these cheerfully, and overcome them tactfully, and contrive to have a smiling welcome for the bread-winner. Could a wife not be trusted to spend sufficiently wisely? If not, does not the mistake lie deeper—in the original choice of a wife? The 'Mere Man' overlooks altogether the possibility of the wife's possessing an income of her own; but perhaps that is beside the question.

"The management of servants is, of course, a serious undertaking, and nothing but experience teaches one the best course to pursue. Doubtless, there is room for much improvement in the training of girls for domestic service, and the desultory way they pick up the little they know is far from an ideal method.

"'A Mere Man' says 'servants are what their mistresses make them.' To a certain extent they may be, and without doubt a good mistress has a large amount of influence over them; but, then, as every mistress is different, and every servant an individual, it is useless to generalise on such a topic. The family circle—particularly in England—is so isolated, that no rules suitable to a factory or a workshop can be of any avail. Each household is a law to itself."

. . . . . .

J. M. starts in a sarcastic vein:—"I am sorry to think of you working hard all day long with only your lunch and your coffee, and your afternoon tea, and your game of dominoes, and your cigars, and your gossips on the Exchange, and your quiet evenings at home to help you on the way. No wonder you nag at your idle wife, who has only to look after her house and her servants and her children, her mending, sewing, altering, contriving, and providing for—oh, good heavens! for *you!* Chops, too! Poor dear! And nothing *but* chops, it would appear; or is it that you don't know the names of the joints? I should insist upon my wife going to the slaughter-house herself, if I were you, and poking the animals in the ribs to see which would make the best 'bran-mash' (I should have said 'thistles!')

"I am afraid you were not very well when you wrote your letter, because three shillings worth of mackerel is rather a large order for a family for whom a pound of salmon would be sufficient. Such an indigestible fish, too. No wonder you are feverish. Don't excite yourself more than you can help, when I tell you that it is the common practice of housekeepers to arrange with the butcher for a certain price 'overhead' for all meat, excluding steak.

"What a nice large coal cellar you have

in your house! It would need hydraulic pressure to get twenty tons of coal into mine, or any other which I have seen in 'middle-class houses.'

"So your wife cried, did she, when you rounded upon her about your penny roll? They must have shed many tears, poor eyes, since you beheld them first! I can understand that the rest of your family prefer stale bread. The servant was sent in secret to procure the roll . . . 'Mere Man,' in that eloquent sentence your portrait is sketched. A three volume novel lies wrapped in those pregnant words. . . . The plot was discovered, and the baker punished. Had you to do without your penny roll during the month of probation? That was hard on you; but never mind, the baker has altered his round, and what a comfort to know that other people have now to wait for their breakfast instead of you.

"'Mere Man,' shall I tell you in brief what I think of you? 'I don't believe there's no sich person!' Your name is Harris. You are a ruse to excite feminine readers, and, as such, receive my congratulations on your success. I know many men, and they have their faults; but all true men share the virtue of loyalty towards the women who love them, and who spend their lives in their service, amidst suffering, weariness, and constant care."

. . . . . .

PETRUCHIO takes up the cudgels for his wife:—"I have had a hard enough task to keep my Katherine's hands off 'A Mere Man' from week to week. With the appearance of his onslaught against a mother's management of her children, the pent-up volume of indignation has overflowed, quite in her old shrewish style. As she has confiscated my latch-key and knocked off all sporting papers until I reply to 'A Mere Man's' mischievous doctrines, I am compelled to undertake the duty of scribe. So here goes.

"Katherine insists that she can not only

'put hand upon her heart and truthfully say' that she knew what 'to do' with our Corisande when the mite brought joy into this household, but she can continue to keep her hand over that organ without flinching and offer priceless advice to parents in general. I can certainly confirm my spouse's assertion that, for some months prior to baby's advent, a perfect library of works, of the 'Advice to Mothers' order, pervaded our residence.

"Prepared indeed! 'This annonymous creature will want to dispute the value of goose oil in cases of croup next,' cries my wife wrathfully. 'A Mere Man!' A mere fool, say I; a crusty old maid or bachelor to boot.

"Katherine is especially incensed over 'A Mere Man's' monstrous ignorance on the subject of short-coating. Every mother worthy of the name knows that a 'three-quartered' costume intervenes between the long and the short periods of infantile draping. As for babies grovelling about in draughts stark-naked, my indignant helpmate considers it a stark-mad idea altogether, only applied to poor little gutter children whom poverty and stupidity impel towards premature dissolution. In fact, she thinks 'A Mere Man's' experiences must be gathered from the slums rather than the well-ordered, middle-class nursery. Katherine adds that she will be happy to demonstrate to *bonâ-fide* visitors the admirable three-quarter system as exemplified on the person of our thriving Corisande."

. . . . . .

A Mere Woman of Waterford does not hesitate to say:—"I agree with the writer, 'A Mere Man,' that a middle-aged, hard-working man does not get, as a rule, sufficient value for his money. His comforts are not, like his income, increasing, and his partner is apt to forget that his are the brains and hands that provide the house, clothes, and good things generally of life to so many.

"Daughters, too, should never forget this.

A mother is apt to think her partner has a great privilege in providing for and educating his children to the utmost extent his income will allow. Either his family should be smaller, or he should educate his girls as well as his boys to provide for themselves. 'A Mere Man' says 'their capacity to do so remains to be proved.' Yet he probably wishes to keep his girls at home and make them do work of some kind to lighten the expenses.

"I may add that though I am a woman, and a housekeeping one too (I ought to be making jam instead of writing this), I quite believe that men on the whole can manage a house and servants and children as well, if not better, than women. *But* they would sooner do something else; so I fancy would some women. In any case they could manage an establishment better than the average woman, whose thoughts are taken up with bicycles, a new way of doing the hair, or converting an orange box and a cracked plate into something for which they were never intended.

"I am looking forward to 'A Mere Man's' further exposure of our blunders, and hope to be able to correct some of mine. I am also anxious to know why his house is not more comfortable than it used to be, though if he expresses his contempt of woman's capacity for this and that as emphatically in his house as in his letter, he does not deserve to be too comfortable."

. . . . . .

These are the views of A MERE WOMAN AND MOTHER:—"In answer to 'A Mere Man' I should say his trumpeter is dead. He speaks of women in three classes—Angels, slum women and cow women. I am sure the sex ought to be highly edified and grateful. As he knew the different classes of women so well, why didn't he choose an angel?

"Paterfamilias owns that he married for love. If he didn't trouble himself about a woman who could manage for him before he was married, why do so now? If he gives love and she returns it, what has he to grumble about? If he married without counting the cost, that's his look-out, not his wife's.

"Again he says: 'My office has improved.' Has he done all the work himself? what about his helpers? Undoubtedly they are good business men, who work and stay with him for the sake of their wives and families. His poor wife, on the other hand, is worried to death to get willing and conscientious helpers even at a high price, as servants are so scarce. They are generally single women who have no one depending on them, and so, in many cases, will not be told how, or what to do, or when to do it. If they cannot have their own way they will leave, as they know they can easily get other places. Not so with his subordinates.

"Again he says 'there should be nothing simpler in the world than to manage a house, a few servants, and a few children,' but 'A Mere

Man' has left out *the master of the house.* Granted men manage restaurants—so they ought—this represents only one branch of woman's work. The poor wife has to see to the supply of provisions for the whole family, arrange for the cooking, and manage the cook—which is the hardest of all.

"Next, about the children. The woman bears them, rears them, always has them with her except when at school or out with the nurse, whom she can't always trust, and when they are grown up they give her more anxiety than when young. What man could shield, guide, and counsel girls like a mother?

"The sum and substance of 'A Mere Man's' grumbling seems to be money. It's a pity he ever loved a woman, for if he had not he might have saved his pounds and had sufficient income to manage some one else's household."

. . . . . .

AN INDIGNANT MOTHER feels that she must rush into print on behalf of her injured sex :—" It seems to me 'A Mere Man' must be most unfortunate in his womenfolk; I am thankful to say I have met very few 'such awful idiots' as he describes in all his articles, and I cannot believe many such exist. I have been married just nine years, and began my married life with one servant and £2 a week to keep house on. I paid all food expenses for four persons and other things, such as oil for lamps, which we always used, newspapers, fares to town, and small things from the drapers, etc. This continued for three years, and during that time we often had visitors stopping with us, and friends to high tea, suppers, etc., etc. Now I have three children and four servants, and am sorry to say, spend £6 a week, and find I cannot do it for less (although nothing is wasted) as we still nearly always have some visitor.

"I always spend an hour or so in my kitchen every morning, seeing to everything, and am thankful to say could earn my living any day as a good plain cook or thorough house or parlourmaid. I can also sing well and play fairly, and for some time earned all my clothes by painting Xmas cards, so you see, although thoroughly useful, I can be a little ornamental as well. I have three dear children and the best husband in the world, and would cheerfully go out *charring* to support them if necessary; but I could be the most horrid of people if I had one of the ridiculous husbands I read and sometimes hear about. A selfish and hateful 'Mere Man' would lead a most unhappy life if I had the misfortune to be his wife; as it is, my dear husband and self are happier in each other's companionship every day we live; we are both fond of music, bicycling, etc., and my husband spends a good deal of his spare time golfing, as he is so much better since he took up this form of exercise.

"He is devoted to his children, and so am I, and I beg to tell 'A Mere Man' that I dine with my children every day, and know every mouthful they eat, and personally attend to their beef-tea every morning, so that it shall be strong and good. My children have everything to make them happy, but they must obey me at once and be polite and kind to all beneath them, and to dumb animals, and although outrageously noisy are very seldom naughty.

"My head nurse has been with me since my eldest boy was six weeks old, and my under nurse four years, my housemaid three years, and my cook only left because family matters obliged her to, so I have now a new one. Of course servants are very troublesome, but we are none of us perfect, and must give and take. 'A Mere Man' said in one of his articles, how is it servants always do things willingly for their master?—what a question! The master is a man, the mistress a woman, the sex question and nothing else! I try to be always *just* before everything, and kind, but must confess that I found out kindness does not always answer with servants.

"The article on children is idiotic; he says,

'I don't believe women have the very slightest idea how children should be taken care of.' Then I must be the brilliant exception, for I use the common sense God gave me, and *do know;* they have always had long sleeves, shetland vests, socks, etc., and flannel pyjamas at night; they are not fed on sweets, but on porridge, fish, good joints, beef-tea, stewed apples, boiled sago, tapioca, milk, etc."

. . . . . .

This is what LEN says:—"Your way of looking upon home as a branch of your business is original; but to require it to show a profit on paper seems to me sheer nonsense. However, taking it in your own way, my opinion is that if the comforts of home have decreased with you, this, to some extent, reflects on yourself—you are the head of the firm, so, if you were as wise and clever as you say you are, your wife and daughters would not be such a poor dunderheaded lot as you make them out to be.

"Women are much more careful in spending money than you give them credit for. Their method of purchasing when they like and where they like is unquestionably a better plan than what you suggest. For instance, if they tied themselves, as you say, to one butcher, they would have less choice; and as to the discount—well, every tradesman must have a reasonable profit, and if you do not pay the proper price, he will have to cheat somebody, and the probability is that you will yourself suffer.

"Neither do women purchase in such out-of-the-way proportions of the various articles required; they plan things out to a much greater nicety than men could do if they had the task to perform. It is generally the caprice of the man at the table that makes the articles served up appear out of proportion.

"Now, Mr. 'Mere Man,' I begin to think you are a very queer stick! After advising that a woman should go to her butcher and get discount for weekly payments, I find that you censure her because she will insist on paying weekly. I don't wonder at your house being a badly-managed one, because, with such an inconsistent head, nobody would know what to be at. I believe women do quite right in buying their household goods, dresses, etc., for cash; the credit system is often the cause of the purchases exceeding the income, and, therefore, sooner or later bringing trouble.

"There may be some little truth in your charge that women love to spend money, and are unable to account for every shilling they spend; but are men any better in these respects?

"Your manner of doling the cash out to the woman is rather mean. Where there is a true wife she has as much right to the money as the man has, and where she is taken into his confidence, and the man treats her properly, she will make a better use of household money than he could."

. . . . . .

ANOTHER PATERFAMILIAS gives his happy experience of the success of women in domestic life :—" I am," he says, " fifty-three years of age ; have been married thirty years ; I have had nine children and four grandchildren, and my long experience has been the exact reverse to everything you assert.

" You first find a specimen, and then violently contend that it is a representative case and a fair example of the whole sex and nation. I have also a right to my opinion, and I assert that my experience is a better, a truer, and more faithful type of the British maid, wife, and matron than the one you have so skilfully delineated.

" You say that ' Your one idea is to be strictly fair to women.' How unfair you are, and have been, I will endeavour to show.

" Take one of your first broad assertions, ' Women have always had the management of the house, and there they fail hopelessly, either to provide comfort or spend money in the "proper way."' This is an abominable libel. The care that women take for the comfort of husbands, homes, and families, their love, patience, industry, and skill, is beyond all praise.

"Let me give you a specimen first of economy. A pretty frock that was obtained for our first baby was worn in succession by all the other *eight* children, and was practically thoroughly well used for over *twenty years.* We have carpets that have been in use twenty-five years, and which are neither dirty or shabby yet.

"Next, a word about cooking. For thirty years meals have always been ready to the moment. Reckoning for an average of eight persons who sit down to four meals a day, the wife provides over 11,000 meals per annum, without ever a single hitch from January to December. Everything is always perfect in quality, cost, cooking, and serving.

"If I want breakfast at six a.m., it is provided and daintily served, without the slightest commotion, even if we had not gone to bed before one o'clock the same morning.

"You mention scornfully the item, 'Coals.' We use the very best and most expensive house coal, and the total expenditure, without any stint, averages *sixpence per day*. We have always a bright, cheerful fire in the kitchen and in the rooms whenever desired.

"You say 'men can teach themselves to cook, and all the rest is child's play.'

"Well, I will give you a challenge—to find in the world *three men* that will do in one day, and do it as well, the work that is done in my house by my wife, now fifty years old, and one of my daughters aged twenty-five, with the assistance of a charwoman, who does not arrive until 8.30.

"At 7 a.m. Fire lighted, boots cleaned, etc.

"By 7.30. Eight persons served with a *preliminary* cup of delicious tea, carried, in several bedrooms.

"By 8.30. All sit down to breakfast, consisting of porridge, bacon, tea, coffee, white and brown bread, toast, cooked tomatoes, etc.

"By 10.30. Beds are made, and bedrooms and other rooms tidied.

"By 12.45. Dinner of roast meat, two vegetables, pudding, cheese, and cups of coffee for those who desire it.

"By 5 p.m. Tea with potted meat (home-made), home-made bread, teacakes, toast, etc.

"By 10 p.m. A light supper.

"Whilst all this is going on, being provided, served, cleared away, pots changed and washed up, these *two delicate and refined ladies wash, wring, dry, mangle, starch*, and *iron* in the *most perfect* manner *four hundred articles* of wearing apparel and household linen, and knead and bake bread and cakes to serve the whole family for three days.

"Then, never forget, from morning till night this tremendous task, which you call 'child's play,' is gone through without a murmur, with cheerfulness and with good nature, the prominent feeling being to get the meals to suit the men and the starched things to their fastidious tastes.

"This I consider a truer type of the British housewife than the types you condemn.

"I know quite well your examples, but they are not representative Englishwomen.

"There are millions of men that are 'mouchers,' 'incompetent duffers,' 'thorough wasters.' It would be as fair for a woman to write an article holding them up as a standard sample of Englishmen as for you to make out your types of incompetent women to represent the English wife."

. . . . . .

KINGFISHER is brief but decided. She says:—"I have read the letters of Paterfamilias with great interest and think that he is wrong upon many points. Being a man, although the father of a family, he cannot know much about housekeeping if, as I suppose by his letters, he is engaged in business. When he says that all discomfort and extravagance of home life is due to the 'Missus,' he is incorrect. Women in this age have something else to do than to stand *behind* their servants all day long, and would not do it if they could. When a mistress engages a new cook or housemaid, if she is a good housekeeper she takes an inventory of everything, both in kitchen, scullery, and pantry. When saucepans are asked for, she tells her cook that there are plenty for her daily use, and does not buy fresh ones. With the housemaid it is the same. New cloths are not needed, nor dust-pans, as in a well-managed home the former are not allowed to be worn into holes and the latter are not without handles. I have been a wife for twenty years, and am sufficiently conceited to think I know something about housekeeping. During that time I have only kept two servants, but I give my stores out every week, and my servants know that they have to make that quantity do. A lady I know very well keeps five servants, and manages her house on the same principle. I must beg to inform Paterfamilias that even in this nineteenth century there are still *some good housekeepers left.*"

. . . . . .

COMMON-SENSE contributes a running fire of comment:—"I should like to point out some of the more glaring discrepancies in your articles. To begin with, you do not state the size of your family. 'Your wife and daughters,' evidently no sons, daughters only, shall we say two, three, or ten? It is impossible to consider the servants' question unless we know the number of the grown-up members of your family.

"'Assets, etc., wife not an improving property.' Are *you* 'an improving property?' is your temper better than it was? etc. 'Any man could manages a house, etc., to greater advantage than any woman.' What is that quotation of some people 'rushing in where angels fear to tread'?—you might look it up. 'O! glorious power of self opinion, for none are fools in thy dominion.'

"'Butchers make no allowance for bone or fat.' Do you think for a single moment that any man could induce a monopolist like a butcher to allow for bone, 'a butcher's fair profit'? There is not such a thing as a fair profit in the butcher's business, for it is said that any butcher who sells a beast a week can live, bring up his family, and drive his gig.

"I was once behind the scenes running a large catering business at a big exhibition in the provinces; the manager, a capable business-like German, could make no impression on the butcher, and you should not expect your wife to do so.

"'Fish—provide three pounds mackerel and won't provide one pound salmon.' The size of your family being omitted, I can only judge that your wife prefers that all the family shall partake of fish, while you evidently want that pound of salmon for your own and her consumption, while the children go without!

"'Cheque for twenty tons of coal paid for in advance.' What an absurd idea! A business man would place a contract or open order for a given weight to be delivered at such a rate per month at a stated price, and pay for it as he got it—'when the blind lead the blind,' etc. Save 5s. a ton indeed; it means simply locking up money for a year in advance, and possibly, if the coal merchant dies or levants, losing your money.

"'Housekeeping money, false pretences, criminal negligence.' What a nice man you are, what a treat for your neighbours! Think it over, old man, and apologise. 'Never saw the saucepans or the stockings.' You imply evidently that your wife never bought them, that it was a mode of thieving. Thank goodness that you have a wife at all, for certainly you don't deserve one. Buying 'half the items that are not pressing,' etc.—

why not say your wife is an absolute fool? it would save time.

"'Paying cash destroys credit,' 'order goods, and when bills come in, pay something on account,'—and this man pretends to be in business for himself. Well, somebody in his office has to take care of him; that is plain enough. He grudges the interest on the money paid in weekly accounts, and would like the money in his business, though he recommends paying the coal merchant in advance. Another Solomon, does he not know that by paying weekly, his wife only pays once for goods got? She can remember a week's trivial items, while 'A Mere Fraud' (I mean 'A Mere Man') himself, if he adopted his own system, would be paying for goods received two or three times over; besides, if he wants to calculate how much his housekeeping costs him, it is all plain: compare one week with another, as far back as he likes, of the different trades-people; and he is, moreover, able to sit and rest at home in an evening without everlasting hearing that 'Mr. So-and-So has brought his bill and is waiting for the money,' as would be the case under his foolish plan. Let 'A Mere Man' take up the fact that the women he accuses of criminal negligence, false pretences, and stigmatises (indirectly) as a thief, has more business acumen than he is possessed of.

"'Nurses get discount on the milk for the nursery, and the cook for kitchen goods.' Evidently 'Mere Man's' nurse pays the milk-man's bills and the cook pays the butcher! 'A little knowledge is a dangerous thing.'

"'Women's mission is to put the blame on someone else; Eve began it.' Really, Mr. 'Mere Man,' if you must write something, do for goodness' sake state facts, for you must know that man, to his eternal shame, began it. He put the blame on Eve—'The woman tempted me and I did eat.' Now he was a 'mere man,' I admit, but it was not a manly way of meeting the case. If there had been any society at all, he would have been hounded out of his club, and sent to Coventry for his meanness; if it had been the other way about, would the woman have split upon the man and blamed it upon him? *No.* I have always been a bit ashamed of Adam—but this is a digression.

"'Bachelors keep their servants for years treasures,' etc., because Bachelor is out two-thirds of his time, they do as they like, and rob him left and right as well.

"'Sulky female servants will do anything for the master or the young gentlemen.' Oh! blind bat, where is your understanding? *Why is this?* you say; why indeed? If you cannot reason that out, you can't expect to shine very much in your domestic aspirations of a perfect home-life with a man at the helm.

"'Servants cost as much as rent and taxes.' Rent you say is £60, taxes one-third, £30, therefore servants cost you £90! Presently we shall learn more, and get you on the hip somewhere else. Speaking of servants, you leave out (evidently you have never heard of it), the German 'Dienst Buch' or service book. Every German servant treasures her service book as a most sacred possession; in it, each employer writes time of arrival, length of service, remarks, etc.; it is a testimony of the servant's age and whole life, and the laws are very stringent about writing only what is true in this book. Something of this sort adopted in England would do an immense amount of good for both servants and mistresses.

"'The blind leading the blind,'—think it over, old chap.

"'Go and watch how a man conducts his business.' I think I shall write a few articles on the absurd systems that occur in a man's business, under-line the weaks points, and let women behind the curtain a bit.

"'Take stock.' Fancy a mere man with his memorandum book. 'Sarah! there were 12 pieces of soap when you came—where are they, Sarah? You cannot have lost them; I am determined they shall be found,' and so on.

"'Volume form,' says a correspondent; yes, by all means, and labelled 'Comic Housekeeper's Manual.'"

. . . . . .

A PLAIN-SPOKEN WOMAN says:—"Nothing can be much worse for a man than to have a dirty wife, and a woman who does not see that her kitchen and larder (the places where all food is prepared) are kept clean must indeed be a dirty woman. Beetles and crickets must abound in such places as you describe your cupboards to be.

"I suppose the wife has brought her daughters up to be the same. Pray do not disclose your identity (at any rate to your friends), or the men will fight shy of your girls, and you will never get them off your hands.

"Now, about that dresser. I think that, if you are familiar enough with the kitchen to go and fetch sticks when a fire is out, you might put on those handles yourself, and so you will, in one short half-hour, save £20."

. . . . . .

A DOMESTIC writes, with some indignation, to say:—"I think 'A Mere Man' wrongly misjudges us servants when he regards servants as thieves, and terms the kitchen as 'thieves' kitchen.'

"In the first instance, he credits us with wastefulness, over-eating, and pilfering. Probably there are some of that class ot girls about, and Paterfamilias seems to have been favoured with a few of them, but the majority of them are not so black as they are painted.

"If a really respectable, honest servant is lucky enough to obtain a good situation, and is treated with respect due to her, the mistress will find her a good servant. 'A Mere Man' credits us with 'waste,' which, perhaps, is true in some cases, where some inexperienced girl is in the kitchen. Secondly, with 'over-eating.' If servants have three good meals a day I think most are satisfied.

"I cannot believe a girl could eat a quarter

of a pound of cheese and half-a-loaf, besides other little dainties from the dinner table, which 'A Mere Man' alludes to, if she has the same amount of food as we have during the day, and then take that amount of supper. She cannot be human, but must be looked upon as a monster.

"Good cooks generally contrive to make the most of everything, instead of demolishing everything that is left from dinner, as 'A Mere Man' credits us with. I have been in some good houses in the West of England, and have made the acquaintance of several cooks, and I have found that where a mistress studies the cook, the cook will look well after the interests of the mistress. Speaking of the stock-pot, I know a cook who has been in one situation for several years. As soon as dinner was over she collected all bones from plates not having been fingered, washed them thoroughly, and put them into the stock-pot. She also clarified all fats and drippings, and used them for frying purposes, and so saved her mistress several pounds a year. I adopted the plan, and no doubt other cooks do the same.

"'A Mere Man' also speaks of us giving to every beggar who comes to the door. I have been in my situation nine years, and can never remember giving away anything unless I have had my mistress's permission to do so.

"I will close by saying if every mistress spoke a little more kindly, and trusted her servant a little more than the average mistress does, there would be a better class of servants about than there are at the present day."

. . . . . .

A Mere Woman, of Crouch End, has small patience with "A Mere Man," and goes for him full tilt:—"I, in common with many other wives and housekeepers, have been looking forward with considerable curiosity from week to week to the articles by 'A Mere Man.' He began by being mildly interesting; one even felt he might chance to be in some degree helpful, for managing a house and the modern domestic is not by any means the simple thing he would have us believe. The second article contained some egregiously foolish suggestions, whilst the third is beneath contempt, it is so evidently a splenetic outburst engendered by his own individual experience, which he foolishly imagines to be that of every other man. I say this in all pity for the poor lady whose hard lot is irrevocably cast in with that of such a narrow-minded, mean-spirited, and ignorant creature. His stinginess alone is painfully apparent. One can quite imagine the scene he himself suggests: the poor, worried wife trying her hardest to obtain a little money for current expenses; the irritable husband grudgingly producing the smallest possible amount, growling because eggs are a farthing more apiece than when he was last called upon, never thinking that while he is haggling over a sixpence, coals may have 'gone up' 2s. a ton, and stone fruit become double its former price.

" He never thinks either of the utter humiliation to any woman of being treated in the way in which he admits to treating his wife. No wonder she yields to the wild temptation of an occasional small luxury. And even the most censorious could scarcely blame her for providing her children with stockings and her kitchen with saucepans. With that type of man every small necessity for the household has to be literally fought for. His ignorance of these subjects is vast, and all sensible men admit this, and put *some* faith in the knowledge and judgment of the woman whom their own choice has placed in the position of manager of their households. What tired city man, on arriving at home and sinking with relief into arm-chair and slippers, would wish to be confronted by an array of kitchen utensils and children's underclothes, whilst his wife carefully explained the price and use of each? Most men I know would say—'What on earth do I know of such things? Get what is needed, but don't bother me.'

"Then, again, the 'Mere Man' blames his partner for her very virtues. One of his wails is that she bought six boxes of soap when he expected her to buy one. Does he not know that it is far cheaper to buy things of this kind in large quantities? Soap especially improves vastly by keeping; it hardens, and is much more economical in consequence. You may say—'Oh, that was only by way of example.' Yes, but if the 'Mere Man' wishes to convince anyone that he knows what he is talking about let him choose his examples with more discretion, and not 'give himself away' so completely.

"At the risk of being diffuse, I must touch upon two or three more points brought forward by this great domestic reformer. One is that women will insist on paying their bills weekly, instead of running long accounts and paying a little every now and then, just to keep the tradesmen's mouths closed. Who but a lunatic would seriously advocate this latter system, if economy were to be the great object aimed at? I fancy that I am right in saying almost every man of limited means would regard the weekly, or at any rate *frequent and regular*, payment of bills as an absolute essential, and look upon the plan of 'A Mere Man' as most pernicious. No one can keep proper track of items on a bill of long standing, and it is a generally understood fact that tradesmen charge less for their goods when they know the money will shortly follow the order. They have repeatedly told me that they find it to their advantage to do this. The 'Mere Man' might well complain if his wife let his accounts run on and on; he would probably end in the Bankruptcy Court if she followed all his fads.

"One thing more. Whose fault is it that girls are ignorant of the management and value of money, as undoubtedly many of them are? Their parents'; their fathers' fully as much as their mothers'. A father very frequently even grudges his girls a dress allowance to manage for themselves, whilst any wish to develop their own life and individuality is, as a rule, rigorously discouraged. The child is taught nothing of book-keeping or domestic economy, and then when she grows up ignorant, her father sneers at her.

"Let men join hand in hand with women in this great cause—insist that their daughters shall be instructed in every useful matter, and fitted for life as boys are; then we shall have better-managed homes, and there will be no more possibility of women having to look for help and instruction to such a 'blind leader of the blind' as 'A Mere Man.'"

. . . . . .

KENMARE does not mince matters. She says:—"I have been much amused in reading your diatribes. Your wife, indeed, must be *very* stupid, and I am sorry for you; but it does not say much for your judgment in choosing such a useless helpmeet. It would be a sorry thing, indeed, for homes in general if all women were of the pattern you describe them. According to you, there is *nothing* women are capable of doing, and everything is possible with men. What would become of thousands of middle-class homes, where only one servant is kept, if the mistress did not personally superintend the household duties in every way? What would happen if waste were allowed when the housekeeping had to be done on a limited sum weekly? Your arguments may apply to a certain class of women whose husbands are well off, and they consequently do not look after the little expenses connected with the keeping up of a home; but they certainly *do not* apply to women generally. Middle-class women have to watch carefully their household bills, and see that everything is made the most of, to make ends meet at all.

"As to your saying men understand the management of children better than women, I consider that absurd. *No one* understands the management of a child better than its own mother. The management of children comes naturally to a woman with motherhood. You cannot lay down rules for this, as every child differs, and needs its own peculiar treatment, the constitutions of no two children being identical."

. . . . . .

BARBARA accepts correction, and quietly turns the other cheek.—"Reformers," she says, "never did have a good time; but it is hardly 'the thing' to abuse you for your well-meant efforts to re-organise the management of our homes.

"Myself, I can acknowledge a lot of truth in your articles; but I have not been a wife very long, and my husband is, of course, the best and dearest man in the world. Of course the management in our small *ménage* is not perfect. The servants *are* extravagant. They are not of the calibre of the 'highly respectable person,' but they bitterly resent correction or remonstrance in its very mildest form. I do maintain that a servant takes more notice of a curt rebuke from a man, than of a gentle and well-meant remonstrance from a woman. I know a man always argues that it is not his place to interfere with affairs of the household, but the fact remains as I have stated. The eternal sex question, you see, arises even in the case of mistress and servant.

"As to the lady who dreads the visit of her husband to the butcher, she must be a careless housekeeper. I thought every woman (where the income is moderate) had a fixed allowance for housekeeping. I think, dear 'Mere Man,' you wrong us just a little. I know several women who have a certain sum allowed for housekeeping, and who never exceed that allowancc, except in cases of entertaining extra guests, in which case, of course, extra allowance is necessary.

"But I thank you for your articles. They are helpful to me, though I don't quite like admitting it. I prefer to be told that all I do is perfection, even though my common sense tells me otherwise."

. . . . . .

SONNY waxes warm and personal. He says:—"I have read with some interest the letter of 'A Mere Man,' and it seems to me that he had better take the advice of a certain gentleman who calls himself a 'Black Philosopher,' and says, 'All you married men had better go and hang yourselves.' He seems to think the world was made for himself alone, and for the special benefit of his money-grubbing propensities. In the opening of his letter he says he married his wife because he loved her.. He has worked all his life for the same cause. Does he slander her because he loves her too? I am not married myself, but I know how my mother has managed our house, loved and cared for us all at home, so I must say a word in her defence. Does your correspondent think, when he sees his family growing up around him, his daughters growing into women, that he has lived in vain? Does he not think that they have a mission in life to fill? Does it not give him some sort of satisfaction to think, 'I have done all I can for them, I trust them, they will never be a reproach to me'? If this is no satisfaction to him it ought to be. And then in his old age. Oh! that is the time he will find his satisfaction. 'I shall always have them round me to comfort me when I am old,' is a thought that is uttered by thousands of fathers and mothers, and it comforts them.

"No! Your correspondent is one of those miserable mortals who sees nothing in any other light but that of gain. Gain is the motive power of his life; but some day he must pay the debt of nature, and then to what use his gold, for he cannot take it with him? He must think all women are fools, and cannot think for themselves. 'They cannot cook,' he says. Now, I am in the city, and go day by day to one of our big restaurants for my lunch, but never have I had anything yet like I get cooked at home, and any sensible woman can cook.

Men do this, and men do the other; but could a man darn his own socks, sew on his own buttons, and do housework? I very much doubt.

"'A Mere Man' had better go to some place far away from the hands of woman, and live entirely by himself, and see how he gets on. The world will go on very well without him."

. . . . . .

CULTRA sends her indignant protest all the way from Ireland, and seems to pour contempt equally on "A Mere Man" and upon the man of her own household.—"It would take the scathing pen," she says, "of a Mrs. Lynn Lynton to shrivel up the arguments as they deserve; but as a housekeeper of some fourteen years' standing, I wish to protest most emphatically and indignantly against the whole tone of 'A Mere Man's' letters.

"I cannot imagine a man, blessed with a wife and daughters, speaking of the one as a 'non-improving property,' and the other as 'mere speculations.' The writer is more likely to be some sour and cynical bachelor, determined to 'take it out of' our unfortunate sex for reasons best known to his unwholesome self. Allowing that he *is* in the unhappy condition of 'A Mere Man,' *whose fault is it but his own?* Why, if he is such a splendid business man does he not see to it that he gets value 'for his money' all round?

"He must be a nice sort of 'molly-coddle who cannot keep a certain portion of his earnings to lay out upon his own amusements, and so rid himself of some of the *bile* that is evidently poisoning his own existence and that of his much-to-be-pitied woman-kind. They would not fret, I am very sure, if the pater took to golfing or cycling, even though it should mean fewer luxuries, or a dress less in the year.

"As to the *natural* shopping capabilities of a man, my experience tells me they are nonexistent. I am, on very rare shopping occasions, favoured by the presence of a man, and this is the sort of thing that goes on :—'Oh, take the lot, they'll come in sometime!' or, 'Why not take the joint as it is? There's only 12 lbs. in it, and it will save you shopping for the rest of the week,' and so on. On the strength of having saved sixpence, a man will be extravagant for a whole week afterwards. This *fact* has been verified by many of my housekeeper friends.

"'A Mere Man' knows nothing, poor ignoramus, of the infinite thought and planning that is going on in the often over-tired brain of the house-mother—thoughts extending into the small hours of the morning, when her superior half is fast asleep and snoring!

"Let 'A Mere Man' keep to *his* part of the bond, and look well to his 'office,' of which he boasts so much, and unless he has drawn a blank in the matrimonial lottery, he will find he has as happy and well-ordered a home as he deserves. Let his sordid, 'value'-loving soul try to soar a little higher above 'bills' and 'cash' and 'discount'; let him try the effect of 'money-giving' in place of 'money-grubbing,' and perhaps, as a reward, this sore feeling, that he is being robbed by his wife, and cheated by his trades-people, will depart from him."

. . . . . .

A corner must be found for the following attempt to wither poor 'Mere Man' with sarcasm:

"AN IGNORANT HOUSE-MOTHER would be greatly obliged to 'A Mere Man' if he would tell her in one of his valuable articles all he knows about the value of a bullock or sheep on the field, what to allow for what she believes the butchers call 'offal,' and the fair proportion for inferior parts, and bone and fat, that she may be able to calculate the proper price for a mutton chop or a pound of rump steak."

. . . . . .

THE CHERUB tries to hit one nail squarely on the head when he says :—" Many people seem to think that there are only two reasons why a man marries a woman. First, they put the mere desire of possession, and secondly, the getting someone who will manage the house. They are both utterly worthless from the point of view of marriage. Any man with a modest income can procure both. But the one thing that money will never buy is the sweet companionship and sympathy of an intelligent woman whom he loves and who loves him. Any couple of average intelligence can get rid of the perfectly sordid details that seem to form the bulk of the average married existence.

" You have said, piteously, that your home does not pay, and show an improving return.

I cannot see that you have put down the main asset at all; if it does not exist, it is indeed a bankrupt concern, and I am sorry for you."

. . . . . .

MATERFAMILIAS THE SECOND writes with flowing pen and ever-increasing indignation:—"I can no longer refrain from taking up the cudgels in defence of my sex. I know that most men imagine that a man could manage the house much better than his wife. If this is true, why is it not more frequently done? and how does it happen that when a man loses his wife he does not manage the house himself, but after, at most, a few months of domestic discomfort and mismanagement, invariably marries again?

"This won't do. Is it in the nature of man to let pass *unused* such an opportunity of *displaying his superior powers?*

"Speaking of clubs and hotels, I have this

on the authority of men that where an hotel is extra comfortable and successful, you will find a woman at the head; but where a man manages, the waste is often exceptionally great.

"'A Mere Man' prefaces his second paper with the statement that a man gets nothing out of his earnings save board and lodging, and these of a very unsatisfactory character, owing to the extravagance and mismanagement of his wife. Speaking from the experience of all my married friends, I take exception to this *in toto*, and remark, Where is the man who does not spend more in sundries—such as cigars, drinks, billiards, golf, etc.—than he allows his wife altogether?

"I pass your correspondent's sarcastic remarks on *cooking* a chop or potato, and will discuss the ability to purchase. I wonder how many butchers could corroborate his statement, and how many would not rather have the husband to deal with than the wife? Though I admit my husband is a fairly sensible and reasonable man, I have simply dreaded his visit to the butcher, knowing that my resources would be taxed, not so much to cook the meat, as to be able to use, without waste, the excessive quantity.

"I am glad 'A Mere Man' got *his* morning roll at the proper time, and took the trouble to fight for it himself; his wife would not grudge him that privilege. In giving her this assistance he shows the most pleasing feature of his character, and if he will cultivate this spirit in other matters belonging to the house, he will cease to find so much fault. Most husbands resent being *asked* to give advice upon domestic affairs, and generally reply, 'Please yourself,' or 'Don't bother me.' Such is my experience.

"May I ask if, when man and wife enter the married state, they start as equal partners?

If so, why should one give a detailed account of expenditure and not the other? Is it not most galling to a woman who has left a home of comfort or ease, or possibly given up a profitable calling (and, believe me, there are many such) to have to *ask* for money at all, much more to be obliged to account for every penny spent?

"It would save much unhappiness if, at the start of married life, every man would make a definite allowance to his wife, according to his means, over which she should have entire control, and be in no way called upon to account for. Surely no average man would choose for his wife a woman he could not trust to that extent.

"'A Mere Man' must have for his wife a woman much to be pitied, and if she is so easily and invariably gulled by trades-people, we may conclude that it is possible for her to have been deceived by him. Poor woman!

If all of us could learn to imitate some of man's strong business habits, and when we go shopping have the forethought to ask each shopkeeper to 'take a drink' *as a preliminary*, we might then hope to make successful business transactions, and if we only knew how to speculate and *lose* we might be the objects of sympathy rather than blame."

. . . . . .

SCOTCH LASSIE sends the following apt quotation from J. M. Barrie:—"She loved him, but probably no woman can live with a man for many years without having an indulgent contempt for him, and wondering how he is considered a good man of business."

. . . . . .

SQUARE BLUE seems to be quite a Blue-beard in his estimate of women. He says:—"As a married man with the experience of twelve years, and the hoary head which has seen forty summers, allow me to endorse the exceedingly practical letter of Paterfamilias. If there is a fault in the communications, it is the entire absence of sentiment, of which we have quite too much in this world. We don't flog our unruly sons or allow the cane to the schoolmaster; we pity and weep over the hardened scoundrels who do not enjoy penal servitude, and in general we give way to an unhealthy sentimentalism. It is therefore refreshing to read the letter of a man who can calmly survey the business side of married life, and tackle the tyrant woman in her own particular domain."

. . . . . .

It would spoil INDIGNANT SLAVEY'S protest to correct or curtail it. She writes:— "If I were a man, I would challenge Paterfamilias to fight, for the dreadful lies he tells about us poor servants, but as I am only a poor slavey, I must be content to express my feelings in words. He shows only too plainly what he *must be*—a man with no sense. If he has to put up with all that he says, why did he marry? that is the question. So he thinks we servants ought to have bread and cheese for supper, does he? and perhaps he thinks that we leave our homes because we don't get enough to eat?—but he makes a great mistake. Now, for instance, go to *any* servant's home, at *any* time, and you can always find plenty to eat; go from there to a lady house, and you will get a tiny cup of tea and a small piece of cake, or two pieces at the outside, but you must not take any more, why, for the sake of etiquette, very soon the gentry will be getting dessert plates with the fruit painted on them, so that the guests can only take a very little. Why we poor things get such a bad name, I can't think, true there are good and bad servants same as there are good and bad of everything. But really I'd scorn to write anything so mean, people who have the money are the last to part with it, I know heaps of mistresses who send their maids out shopping because they get them cheaper, in places where *they* would not like to be seen themselves. So Paterfamilias need not talk about their being extravagant, men are by far the most so, how much they spend a year on cigars etc., I should not say, enough I should say to keep half a dozen servants. I remember a mistress writing a few weeks back that a servant cost £50 to £60 a year, she put £4 4 0 for wear and tear of the bed clothes as if we went upstairs for the express purpose of destroying the bed, instead of getting into it. I defy any one mistress to say she spends so much on a servant. It is really shameful the way you talk, of eating ourselves sick, and indeed you make a great mistake if you think that we are going to eat all the pieces, we get proper food at home and we want it away from home, in fact I wouldn't lower myself to *do it*, you nasty mean old thing. Change places with one of us, do you think you would like to be so talked about when you didn't deserve it, and I think that the ladies who *have* had good servants, are very mean not to speak up for us, but stop, perhaps it would be a breach of etiquette to do so.—INDIGNANT SLAVEY."